PROVERBS

PROVERBS

Jacques B. Doukhan

Pacific Press®
Publishing Association

Nampa, Idaho | Oshawa, Ontario, Canada
www.pacificpress.com

Cover design by Gerald Lee Monks
Cover design resources from Lars Justinen
Inside design by Kristin Hansen-Mellish

The author assumes full responsibility for the accuracy of all facts and quotations as cited in
this book.

You can obtain additional copies of this book by calling toll-free 1-800-765-6955 or by
visiting http://www.adventistbookcenter.com.

Library of Congress Cataloging-in-Publication Data:

Doukhan, Jacques.
  Proverbs / Jacques B. Doukhan.
    pages cm
  ISBN 13: 978-0-8163-5575-4 (pbk.)
  ISBN 10: 0-8163-5575-4 (pbk.)
  1. Bible. Proverbs—Criticism, interpretation, etc. I. Title.
  BS1465.52.D68 2014
  223'.706—dc23
                              2014022909

July 2014

Contents

Introduction

More than ever before, the world and the church need to hear the voice of Proverbs: "The fear of God is the beginning of wisdom." This message is the book's motto (1:7; 9:10; 15:33; 31:30). Without "the fear of God," without the revelation from above and the active presence of God, wisdom is impossible. The church needs to remember that without the discipline of wisdom, without the imperative of ethics and the effort of thinking, religion has no value. Our societies and our families need to meditate on the words of this book, which reminds us of the reality of truth and which bends us under the duty of righteousness in a world that has lost its reference points.

The book

The book of Proverbs is located in the third part of the Hebrew Bible ("the Writings": Hagiographa), more precisely between the Psalms and the book of Job. Taking the first letter of the name of each of those three books, the ancient rabbis shaped the Hebrew word *'emet,* meaning "truth."[1] The intention of this wordplay was to teach that, although these books are not a part of the Torah (the first five Books of Moses)

---

1. The Hebrew names of those three books are *'Iob* (Job), *Mishley* (Proverbs), and *Tehilim* (Psalms).

7

and are not the words of a prophet, they are still messages of divine truth. The book of Proverbs is intended to teach us how to live all that we've learned in the Torah and in the prophets.

The book of Proverbs is universal. Significantly, all human categories are represented in the book: the poor (10:15b; 14:31; 13:23), the rich (10:15a; 18:11), the wise (21:22; 24:5), the fool (12:15; 26:11), parents and children (19:13), the old and the young (17:6), the king (21:1; 25:2), the servant (14:35; 29:19), the man (20:6) and the woman (11:22; 14:1), husband (31:23) and wife (12:4; 31:10), father and mother (10:1), the Israelite (1:1; 25:1), the non-Israelite (30:1; 31:1), the religious person (15:8), the agnostic (30:3–4), the righteous (10:20), and the wicked (13:25).

This book also deals with all circumstances of life: when we eat (17:1) and when we drink (20:10), when we are sick (18:14), when we work (14:23; 22:29) and do business (11:1), when we do nothing (6:10), when we love (10:12b; 17:17) or hate (10:12a; 26:24), when we relate to people (25:9), when we quarrel (26:20–22), when we speak (21:23) or keep silent (11:12; 17:28), when we teach (13:24; 22:6), when we sleep (4:16; 20:13), when we wake up (6:22), when we think (16:26; 23:17), when we are sad (15:33), when we are joyful (15:13), when we laugh (1:26; 14:13), when we live (7:2), and when we die (5:5; 11:7).

The form

The form of "proverbs" fits perfectly the purpose and destination of the message. Indeed, God speaks here the language of the men and the women who live in the world. It is not the absolute tone of the Law or the sublime oracle of the prophet; it is a vulgar proverb, the same kind as the one we hear in the marketplace, in the street, or in the kitchen. It is brief and catching.

The Hebrew term *mashal,* translated "proverbs," means "to be like," implying the idea of comparison, and it covers a broad variety of literary forms and literary devices. Parallelisms, metaphors, plays on words, rhythms, humor and ironies, antitheses, and riddles are used to capture the great diversity of situations and touch many kinds of sensitivities.

Introduction

The proverb can be a simple saying that sounds like a slogan encouraging a certain ethical attitude: "When you sit down to eat with a ruler . . . put a knife to your throat" (23:1, 2); "A merry heart does good, like medicine" (17:22). It can be an admonition that urges for an action to take place: "Commit your works to the LORD, and your thoughts will be established" (16:3); or it can be a didactic poem designed to provide specific ethical instruction: "Better is a dry morsel with quietness, than a house full of feasting with strife" (17:1). It is often a parable inspired by nature: "Go to the ant, you sluggard! Consider her ways and be wise" (6:6). It may also be a wisdom poem that conveys truth in the form of a parable: "Wisdom has built her house, she has hewn out seven pillars . . ." (see 9:1–9; cf. 8:22–36).

The author(s)

The multifold character of the book is reinforced by its diversity of authors. It is, first of all, the work of King Solomon himself. Although most critical scholars suggest a late dating, many evidences point instead to an early first-millennium date and give support to the traditional attribution to that king.

First, the book of Proverbs explicitly refers to Solomon (1:1; cf. 10:1, 25:1). Outside of Proverbs, the Bible portrays Solomon as a king particularly interested in wisdom (1 Kings 4:29–34; Pss. 72:1; 127:1; Matt. 12:42) and specifies that "he spoke three thousand proverbs" (1 Kings 4:32). The book of Ecclesiastes confirms the same tradition, that Solomon "pondered and sought out and set in order many proverbs" (Eccles. 12:9).

Outside of the Bible, Egyptian literature testifies to the existence of parallel literary currents, which precede or are contemporary to Solomon. One of the most striking observations concerns the Egyptian "Instruction of Amenemope," which contains many significant linguistic, thematic, and stylistic parallels, especially with the third section of the book of Proverbs.[2]

---

2. See James B. Pritchard, ed., *Ancient Near Eastern Texts Relating to the Old Testament* (Princeton: Princeton University Press, 1969), 421–424.

Interestingly, Solomon's wisdom is compared to the wisdom of Egypt: "Thus Solomon's wisdom excelled the wisdom of all the men of the East and all the wisdom of Egypt" (1 Kings 4:30). Solomon's wisdom was so great that "men of all nations, from the kings of the earth who had heard of his wisdom, came to hear the wisdom of Solomon" (1 Kings 4:34; cf. 1 Kings 10:23–24). The Bible reports one of these occasions, when the queen of Sheba, a country situated south of Egypt, came to visit Solomon in order to learn from his wisdom (1 Kings 10:1–13). It should therefore not be surprising to find echoes of Solomon's wisdom in ancient Egyptian literature.

This literary connection with foreign wise men is acknowledged in the book of Proverbs, which refers to non-Israelite authors, including a woman (31:1), in a broad sense under the general expression of "wise men" (22:17; 24:23); or it even refers to them specifically with their names (30:1). The inspired writer did not despise foreign wisdom insofar as it was in agreement with his inspired message. This attitude of humble openness was, in fact, a sign of his wisdom. This method was also an intelligent strategy to reach out to all human types, precisely because his message was universal.

Unfortunately, Solomon's success went to his head. Significantly, the report of Solomon's great popularity among the nations is followed by the report of Solomon's failure, suggesting that his fame because of his wisdom led to personal troubles. Immediately after having praised Solomon for his unsurpassed wisdom, "which God had put in his heart" (1 Kings 10:24) and which was recognized by "all the earth" (1 Kings 10:23–25), the author of the book of Kings notes that Solomon began gathering chariots and horsemen especially from Egypt (1 Kings 10:26–29) and "loved many foreign women, including the daughter of Pharaoh" (1 Kings 11:1). As a result, Solomon erred away from the Lord (1 Kings 11:3–8). Paradoxically, Solomon lost his wisdom because of his wisdom. This information, while confirming Solomon's familiarity with foreign wisdom, suggests that the book of Proverbs was written before his fall from grace, at a time when he was still in full possession of his wisdom.

Introduction

According to Jewish tradition, Solomon wrote the Song of Songs when he was young, Proverbs when he was mature, and Ecclesiastes in his old age (*Song Rabbah.* 1:11).

The structure

The structure of Proverbs reflects the multiplicity of authors. The identity of the various authors is revealed from the outset, in the superscription of each section:

- "The Proverbs of Solomon the son of David, king of Israel" (1:1)
- "The Proverbs of Solomon" (10:1)
- "The words of the wise [ones]" (22:17)
- "Things also belong to the wise [ones]" (24:23)
- "Proverbs of Solomon which the men of Hezekiah . . . copied" (25:1)
- "The words of Agur the son of Jakeh" (30:1)
- "The words of King Lemuel . . . which his mother taught him" (31:1)

Each section has a specific concern:

Section I (1:1–9:18): bad women, and exaltation of "wisdom"
Section II (10–22:16): human relationships and strong religious character (references to YHWH)
Section III (22:17–24:22): parallels with Egyptian literature; ethics and leadership
Section IV (24:23–34): partiality and laziness
Section V (25:1–29:27): leadership
Section VI (30:1–33): skepticism and relationship with God
Section VII (31:1–31): bad women and wine, and the ideal woman (cf. Section I)

The thematic connections and echoes between the various sections suggest a possible chiastic structure overarching the whole book: Section I // Section VII (wisdom, woman); Section II // Section VI (relationship with humans and God); Section III // Section V (leadership); Section IV (partiality and laziness: center of the chiasm).

Method

The challenge in the book of Proverbs is its discontinuity. The connection from one proverb to the next is not always clear. Yet Proverbs is skillfully and intentionally constructed. There is a leading line crossing the whole book and a conducting thought behind the sequence of sayings. This interconnectedness testifies to the inspiration of the biblical text. In this look at Proverbs—where we will pay close attention to key words and other literary clues—the text will not come out as a mere literary collection of interesting wisdom. Instead, through these riddles and poems, our God speaks, and, as a result, profound and extremely relevant lessons strike at the heart of our existence and even hit at some sensitive symptoms of our sick civilization.

The Choice of Life

While in Qohelet (Ecclesiastes), Solomon's other book, the author is presented as king of Jerusalem (Eccles. 1:1), in Proverbs he is introduced as "king of Israel" (1:1). The reason for this slight variation is that when he composes this book, Solomon is still in control of the great kingdom. Solomon has not yet reached the stage when he does not "fully follow the Lord, as did his father David" (1 Kings 11:6). Solomon is still in full possession of his wisdom. And still in touch with his spiritual roots, Solomon decides to transmit his heritage and instruct his son, the future king, just as did the ancient Egyptian kings with their sons. The first lesson follows the progression of a classic curriculum. After having outlined the program and defined the purpose of his course, Solomon lays down the foundation: the fear of the Lord.

Program and purpose

Solomon the Teacher proposes five objectives: "to know wisdom" (1:2a); "to perceive the words of understanding" (1:2b); "to receive the instruction of wisdom" (1:3); "to give prudence to the simple" (1:4); and "to understand a proverb" (1:6).

The first proposition, "to know wisdom," warns us that wisdom is not something that we can achieve by ourselves. The Hebrew verb *yd'*, "to know," refers to the conjugal experience (Gen. 4:1; 38:26); it is often used to characterize the relationship with God (Hos. 13:5; John 17:3).

According to Solomon, "to know wisdom" means first of all to live in a personal relationship with God. "To know wisdom" means "to know God." It is interesting to note that the language of our passage echoes the language of the story of Solomon when he asked God for wisdom (1 Kings 3:7–14). The first verb, *bin*, "to perceive," is precisely the object of his request to God: "Give to Your servant an understanding heart to . . . discern [*bin*] between good and evil" (1 Kings 3:9). The Hebrew verb *bin* is etymologically related to the preposition *beyn*, which means "between," implying the operation of distinguishing between two options or two ways. Wisdom is thus defined as the capacity "to discern," "to distinguish" between good and evil.

Yet this wisdom can be obtained only as a gift from God. The verb "give" (*ntn*) is used three times: the first time by Solomon, who asks God to "give" him the wisdom (1 Kings 3:9); and the other two times by God, who is the subject of the verb (1 Kings 3:12, 13; cf. 1 Kings 4:29; 5:12). The verb "give" appears also in our passage of Proverbs (1:4), where it is associated with the verb "receive" (1:3). In his introduction, Solomon insists that wisdom is "received" from God and is not the result of our work; it is not something we produce.

The book of Proverbs begins with this affirmation of the grace of God. Only through this gift from God shall we be wise. Interestingly, the verb "understand" (*bin*) reappears in the conclusion of our passage; this time the verb applies to the "understanding" of the proverbs (1:6). This is the point of this introduction: before we read the book of Proverbs and try to decipher its message, we need to realize that without God's gift of wisdom, we will not be able to "understand" this book. The proverb will remain "an enigma," and the words of the wise man will be as "riddles" (1:6).

Of course, this wisdom is not some kind of magic formula; it is not just information that we shall "know" in our common-sense understanding of the term. To know wisdom is to know God; that is, it is to have a personal relationship with Him. Solomon insists that unless we "receive" Him, we will not understand Him. Unlike the classic pastoral sermon, which ends with an appeal to repent and draw near to God after a lengthy emotional and/or intellectual development, the book of Proverbs begins with an appeal to receive God in our lives.

The foundation

Solomon had started his teaching with reference to knowledge (1:2). He next explains that the beginning of knowledge is "the fear of the Lord" (1:7). This is the foundation upon which the rest of his lessons will stand. This idea is expressed not only through the syntax of the phrase, which has "the fear of the Lord" at the beginning of the sentence (a sign of emphasis), but is explicitly qualified as "the beginning."

The Hebrew term for "beginning," *re'shit,* refers to the absolute beginning that characterizes creation (Gen. 1:1). This is the meaning that has been retained in Proverbs (see 8:23). The "fear of the Lord" is not just the beginning of a particular religious or intellectual experience; it is the cosmic beginning that encompasses "all" (John 1:3); "all," including the most trivial and ordinary things of daily life; "all," including the most obscure moments when no one sees us. There is no room here for a neutral place, a no man's land between God and humans.

This view is already contained in the very notion of "the fear of the Lord." The fear of God is not some superstitious apprehension often associated with a religious person who obeys God out of fear for his life or for his happiness. To fear God means to have and entertain the acute sense of His presence. God is present not only in the church or when we pray but in the office, in the kitchen, in the bedroom, in the marketplace. God is present when we are with people or when we are alone, in the light or in the darkness (see Ps. 139:2–8). This notion is not to be perceived as a threat. God is not the policeman who watches us in order to catch us and punish us. Instead, as the psalmist understands, this presence of God is a comforting assurance: "You have hedged me behind and before, and laid Your hand upon me" (Ps. 139:5). God's presence means God's protection.

On the other hand, that same notion allows God to be the Judge. Because God can see everything, He can be the just Judge (see Ps. 139:1, 23–24). In Ecclesiastes, Solomon concludes with a call to "fear God. . . . For God will bring every work into judgment, including every secret thing, whether it is good or whether it is evil" (Eccles. 12:13–14). To be aware of God's presence always and everywhere obliges us to a certain way of life inspired and oriented according to God's will, a holy life. This is the lesson that Solomon embraces in his book of Proverbs. The statement, "the fear of the Lord is the beginning of knowledge," means that all venues of life should be rooted in the fear of the Lord. The topic of the book of Proverbs concerns, then, our destiny.

This is why the next point is about education. To ensure the success of this ambitious program, Solomon does not point to the pastor or to the rabbi or the priest or to the professor or to the specialized educator, or to the government. Education is primarily a family affair. Both the father and the mother are involved (1:8–9). This principle frames the book of Proverbs, which begins with the instruction of the father to his son (1:8) and ends with the instruction of the mother to her son (31:1). Solomon entrusts the foundation to the parents' hands. The ornaments and the chain symbolize the beauty and grace of wisdom (3:1, 22). For it is in the family that the son will be prepared to make the right choice, resist the bad influence, and engage in the ways of wisdom.

The call of sinners

The sinners come always in plural (1:10). They like to be in a crowd; the number gives legitimacy and power to their empty cause. They are also described as working "secretly" (1:11, 18) and in haste (1:16), for their intentions are harmful. Their invitation sounds very tempting, suggesting that we will be rich and great (1:13).

Solomon's first advice is simple: "Do not consent" (1:10). The

Hebrew phrase is more concrete; it means literally "do not come!" The same counsel will be repeated later: "Do not walk in the way with them, keep your foot from their path" (1:15). Do not even play with the idea that as long as you refrain from the actual evil, it is OK. Solomon traces the beginning of the mistake as being in the company of sinners. Interestingly, only when we have made that first passive act, not to move, are we able to grasp Solomon's explanation as to why we should not respond to the sinners. The thinking process intervenes only after the gut response of faith and obedience without thinking. Solomon's reason is concerned, then, with the consequence of sin. In fact, evil is not beneficial, for the sinner will be the victim of his own sin. He will fall in his own trap (1:18). The gain that he intended to acquire through his evil work will turn out to be fatal to him (1:19).

The call of wisdom

The call of Wisdom contrasts to the call of sinners. While the sinners speak in plural, Wisdom speaks in singular. It is also interesting that the one who responds positively to Wisdom is singular (1:33), while the fools and the simple ones who reject her invitation are plural (1:22, 24, 28–32). While the sinners hide and work in secret, Wisdom has nothing to hide and shouts in the open (1:21). Wisdom is also obliged to cry because of the "noisy streets" (1:21, NASB). The loud call of Wisdom dismisses any possible excuse of ignorance on the part of the fool. They are well informed about her message: "I will make my words known to you" (1:23). And yet they mock her and despise her call and her invitation (1:22, 24–25). While the lesson about sinners takes only a few verses (1:1–19), Solomon's attention to Wisdom covers most of the book. For the best method to fight against evil is not so much the apologetic demonstration against it, but rather to show the value of Wisdom.

The case takes the form of a beautiful poem in the form of a chiastic structure. The climax of Wisdom's defense is Wisdom's laughter, which is located in the center of the chiastic passage (1:26–28). The mocking irony of Wisdom responds to the mockery of the fools. Wisdom had promised them that she would fill them with her spirit (1:23). Instead, the fools are filled with their own fables. This ridiculous condition of the fools, who refused to listen to Wisdom, is Wisdom's best argument against the foolishness of their choice. This paradox can be observed today in our secular societies, where the majority of citizens mock the minority of believers in God and treat them as naïve. Ironically these "intelligent" and "rational" people, who cannot accept the idea of God, end up believing in all kinds of fables they have invented themselves. They mock those who fear God, but they fear the black cat or carefully avoid passing under the ladder or tremble at the number thirteen. In the same vein are those who offer no doubt about the very imaginative system of evolution, which teaches us that humans are the natural descendants of the chimpanzee or of the little fish, but raise all their doubts against the truth of creation, which brings the most compelling evidence, namely that humans have been created by a powerful Creator.

The response to wisdom

To the previous double warning consisting of two ifs ("if sinners entice you" [1:10], "if they say" [1:11]), which entailed the categorical negation "do not" (1:10, 15), the author of Proverbs proposes three ifs: "if you receive my words" (2:1); "if you cry out for discernment" (2:3); "if you seek her as silver" (2:4). This time the "if" leads to a positive promise: "Then you will understand the fear of the LORD" (2:5). The acquisition of "the fear of the LORD," which is "the beginning of wisdom," is not the result of effort on our part. The only condition for it is our passion, our sincere desire to "receive," "to cry out for it," "to seek." It is not the result of our work; it is, on the contrary, the response of our consciousness of our need, precisely because we are unable to produce it and find it by ourselves. It does not come from us. It is a gift of God: "the LORD gives wisdom" (2:6).

To be wise means simply to put ourselves in God's hands. He will do the job. He will guide our lives: He will shield (2:7), He will guard (2:8a), He will preserve (2:8b). From that experience we will then "understand" (2:9). If we have the wisdom to entrust Him with our life, we will then understand that indeed this choice was Wisdom. We will understand that it was right only if we do the right. The proof of Wisdom will be found in our lives (Matt. 12:33).

From the call to "receive" Wisdom (2:1) the teacher moves to the next step: "when wisdom enters your heart" (2:10). The experience with Wisdom is not just the knowledge of the truth; it is not enough simply to know about the right way. This knowledge must go inside us. The Law of God should be in our heart in such a way that doing God's will becomes pleasant and enjoyable (2:10). It is no longer the product of our painful duty. Only this intimate experience will protect from evil. The outcome of our fight against evil is decided in our heart. As long as we content ourselves with legalistic doing or not doing, overlooking the hidden and secret ripples of our intimate thoughts, we are vulnerable prey to the enemy.

Solomon warns his son against two persons who represent "the way of evil" (2:12): the perverse man (2:12–15) and the seductress (2:16–19). Both look friendly and lovely, but both lead to the same ways of "darkness" (2:13) and "death" (2:18). Both are deceptive. The former takes us away from the paths of righteousness and disguises evil under the face of happiness (2:13, 14). The latter disguises evil under the face of beauty and love, and makes us forget the covenant of our youth (2:17).

The conclusion (2:21–22) recasts the classic doctrine of the two ways. In regard to good and evil, there is no middle way. It is life for the righteous (2:21) and death for the wicked (2:22). This paradigm echoes Moses' appeal to his people in the book of Deuteronomy: "See, I have set before you today life and good, death and evil. . . . I have set before you life and death . . . ; therefore choose life, that both you and your descendants may live" (Deut. 30:15–19).

The prospect of life

The lesson of the choice of life, which was only implied in the preceding verses, is now explicitly inferred in the following chapter, where the motif of "Life" is dominant. It recurs as a refrain (3:2, 7, 16, 18, 22, 23, 35) around five topics, which are arranged according to a chiastic structure (A-B-C-B$_1$-A$_1$): the Law, the Lord, Wisdom, the Lord, the Law.

The Law (3:1–4). The first promise of life is introduced by the negative injunction, "do not forget" (3:1), which responds to the other negative injunction, "do not consent" (1:10). While in the former injunction refusal was expected, in the present injunction acceptance is expected. The duty to remember is generative of life, just as the root of the plant is necessary for its life. For Proverbs, the memory of the Law (3:1) will guarantee long life and *shalom* (3:2), which means "completeness," implying "peace" and "health." The invitation to bind the Law around the neck (3:3) recalls Moses' recommendation about the Law (Deut. 6:8). The Law is described (3:3) with the rigorous dimension of truth (*'emet*) and the lovely dimension of grace (*khesed*).

Grace is not against the Law; it is a part of it, just as justice is. This twofold dimension of the Law reappears in its double effect: "find favor and high esteem" (3:4). The Hebrew word *khen* (translated "favor") means "grace" (1:9; 3:34). The Hebrew word *sekhel* (translated "esteem") refers to the demands of intelligence and the intellectual process and is thus often translated "understanding" (13:15; 16:22; Ps. 111:10).

Again the Law refers to both the dimension of love and the dimension of rightness. The Law applies to both our relationship with God and our relationship with man (3:4b). The same lesson is given in the Decalogue, whose first part (Exod. 20:1–7) concerns our relationship with God and the third part (Exod. 20:12–17) concerns our relationship with our fellow human beings. The section on the Sabbath, which is in the middle (Exod. 20:8–11), concerns both relationships.

The Lord (3:5–12). The obedience to the Law should be rooted in our trust in the Lord (3:3), our faith in God; otherwise we fall into legalism. We do not obey the Law because we judge this Law as good but because the Giver of the Law is good. The value of the Law is not determined by our understanding (3:5) or our wisdom (3:7), an attitude deemed as foolish and hopeless (26:12), but because it is the Law of God.

When Solomon urges his son to "trust in the LORD," it means to "acknowledge" Him "in all your ways" (3:6), which refers to all the aspects of life. And when he exhorts his son to "fear the LORD," it means to "depart from evil" (3:7). To be sure, many people do good things and are ethical even though they do not believe in God, simply because they have received a good education and also because they have learned that it is reasonable to observe these laws for their own benefit.

For the believer there is a more profound reason than just reason itself. The believer's motivation is rooted in his/her relationship with a living person, God Himself. This is why the believer has to "honor the Lord" also with their "possessions" (3:9), which means to give to Him their tithes and offerings, because they know that they owe everything to God. It is, then, just logical that they will be benefit from Him all the more; for to give to God from everything they have is to acknowledge that they have received everything from Him.

Our text goes even further in this reasoning. Even when we endure God's punishment, we should learn to receive it as a gift of God. This is just another expression of His fatherly love and thoughtful concern for us (3:11–12).

Wisdom (3:13–18). In the center of the chapter the author has inserted a poetic hymn to Wisdom. After the rigorous argumentation, poetry should touch another chord to reach all the sensitivities and all the sides of our brain. The poem begins and ends with the same blessing, as an inclusio:

> "Happy is the man who finds wisdom" (3:13)
> "Happy are all who retain her" (3:18)

The two statements respond to and complement each other: it is not enough to find wisdom; we also need to keep it.

Between the two blessings, the value of wisdom is suggested through two metaphors. First, Wisdom is compared to silver, gold, and rubies (3:14–15), to riches and honor (3:16), to affirm the superiority of Wisdom over all these precious things. Second, Wisdom is associated with *shalom* (3:17) and is identified with life (3:18). It is interesting that the former value is held in Wisdom's left hand (3:16b), while the latter value is held in her right hand (3:16a). What this means is that life is more important than wealth.

In fact, the Hebrew reference to Wisdom is related to the tree of life, with which Wisdom is identified (3:18). This last imagery takes us into the midst of the Garden of Eden (Gen. 2:9), which suggests the lost ideal environment when evil had not yet affected the world. At the same time, this evocation from the far past nurtures our hope that one day, in the future, we shall eat the fruit of the tree of life again (Rev. 22:2).

The Lord (3:19–26). The Hebrew wisdom does not exist apart from God; He used it as an instrument to create the world (3:19–20). Thus all the benefits of Wisdom do in fact originate in God, the Creator. The immediate lesson is that our life is in God's hands. Walking with God means, then, a life assurance (3:22) and the guarantee that we will be secure and safe (3:23). Even when we sleep, God is in control (3:24). We should not be afraid (3:24, 25) or worry: "your sleep will be sweet" (3:24b). God will protect us not only from the wicked (3:25a), the external enemy, but from ourselves as well (3:23, 26b).

The Law (3:27–35). Strangely, God does not require anything from us in exchange for His protection. The only duty that God expects from us concerns our neighbors. The same extraordinary religion is outlined in Micah the prophet: "He has shown you, O man, what is good; and what does the Lord require of you, but to do justly, to love mercy, and to walk humbly with your God" (Mic. 6:8).

This is the program of Proverbs: we should not refrain from doing "good" to the one who is in need (3:27); we should not lie to our neighbor (3:28); we should act justly (3:30, 33) and love mercy (3:31); we should be humble (3:34). All these human duties are given in the form of divine commandments. Five times the injunction "do not" is repeated, echoing the "do not" introduced previously in reference to the law (3:1).

These acts on behalf of our neighbor are religious acts not only because they are God's commandments but also because the doing or not doing generates God's blessing or curse (3:33). Again the doctrine of the two ways is delineated. The chapter ends with the perspective of two destinies, "glory" to the wise, "shame" to the fool (3:35). These two words do not refer to a mere psychological condition. Their association has eschatological significance (Hos. 4:7). Along the same line of life and death associated with the righteous and the wicked looms the prospect of eternal life with the glory of God and eternal death in the shame of the dust (Dan. 12:2).

CHAPTER 2

The Path of Life

It is not enough for us to have understood. We have to live according to what we have understood.

There is a story about a man who found a wonderful trumpet in the market. The salesman boasted its magic qualities: "This trumpet," he said, "has a wonderful power; it can extinguish any fire. You just blow into it, and immediately the fire will be mastered." The man was interested and bought the trumpet. As soon as he arrived home he decided to try the magic of the trumpet. He set his house on fire and then started to blow into the trumpet. Unfortunately, and to his bewilderment, the fire kept burning, and the trumpet had no effect on it.

Desperate, he ran to the market and caught the salesman who had sold the trumpet. He complained to the salesman about the trumpet, which was not working and did not perform the promised miracle. The salesman then explained that the function of the trumpet was not to put out the fire but to warn that there was a fire and then people would come and put out the fire. The man went away pondering the lessons of this incident and the foolishness of his action.

Hearing about the truth will not change anything unless we apply that truth to our life. Many people behave just as this foolish man did. They attend church services regularly. They listen day after day,

Proverbs

Sabbath after Sabbath, to the sound of the trumpet. They are well informed about all the beliefs, are zealous about them. And yet, they never change their life; and the fire keeps burning, destroying their house. The operation of hearing includes the performance of doing what has been heard.

This is the message of Proverbs. In this lesson, the call to hear is followed by the call to walk. According to this lesson of Proverbs, the hearing of wisdom will invade all the domains of life.

The hearing assignment

The appeal of the book of Proverbs reminds us again of the fundamental appeal of the book of Deuteronomy: "Hear, O Israel" (Deut. 6:4). There also, as in our passage of Proverbs, the act of hearing belongs to a teaching assignment that takes place in the family context: "You shall teach them diligently to your children" (Deut. 6:7). Home is the first place where we will learn to hear, the first place of education.

Proverbs includes three generations in that process. Education includes past, present, and future. The speaker refers to his children (4:1), to himself as "father" (4:1) and to his own father (4:3), without forgetting the mother (4:3). The educator is thus described as someone who transmits what he has received. We cannot educate ourselves. Education requires that we learn from someone else, someone who is older than us, who knows better than we do. This principle is needed nowadays in these times of distance education and the Internet, which promotes independent education. Although valuable, this contribution should not replace the direct and personal implication of the parent. The lesson focuses, then, on the nature of hearing. Before hearing, we should learn how to hear.

First, we need to realize the value of what we hear. Most students are sent to classes to learn topics that they deem of no value. They attend classes, but their mind and interest are elsewhere. They learn just to obtain the grade and to get their degree.

Proverbs warns against this approach. Unless wisdom is one's priority and passion, one will not hear it. This is why the basic principle of learning is that we need to learn. We should learn with the purpose of retaining the lesson. This counsel is repeated several times: "retain my words" (4:4a); "keep my commands" (4:4b); "do not forget, nor turn away" (4:5); "do not forsake her" (4:6). Learning is valuable insofar as we retain what we learn. A Hebrew proverb compares the one who learns and does not review to someone who sows and does not reap (*Babli. Sanhedrin* 99a). For that purpose it is imperative that we love wisdom (4:6b). Learning without passion will lead nowhere. We will not only take a long time to remember the lesson, we will forget it very quickly.

Wisdom is identified as *re'shit,* "the principal thing" (4:7a). The word has already been used to qualify the "fear of the LORD" (1:7). Unless we consider wisdom as our first choice, we will not learn from it. Proverbs goes even further. Wisdom should be not only our primary option but should be present in all our options (4:7b). Wisdom becomes a way of life.

No wonder the acquisition of wisdom will lead to success, honor, glory (4:8–9), and a long life (4:10). Indeed, Wisdom will inspire us not only in our choice of the "right paths" (4:11) but will protect us and preserve us from stumbling on these paths (4:12).

In conclusion, the teacher says, "Keep her, for she is your life" (4:13), implying that outside of Wisdom, death is expected. It is either life with Wisdom or death without her. This dualistic view is a corollary to the great-controversy drama. There are two ways only. The way of the wicked is the way of evil (4:14), always threatening (4:15–17) and full of darkness. On the other hand, the way of Wisdom is full of light (4:18). While the wicked lives in the night, stumbling on the stones he does not see, the wise man lives in the day and is wide awake, fully aware of the possible dangers (4:18–19).

The next point is about the quality of hearing. The father urges his son to "give attention" (4:20). The acquisition and the preservation of wisdom require concentration. We need to "incline" our ear. This language sounds awkward today considering the effort that is made to meet the student where they are in order to awaken them from sleepiness. According to this methodology, it is the student who should move and strive toward the teacher, not the other way around.

This was not always Jesus' approach. "When Jesus saw great multitudes about Him, He gave a command to depart to the other side" (Matt. 8:18). Those who wanted truth had to seek it. Then "a certain scribe came and said to Him, 'Teacher, I will follow You wherever You go' " (Matt. 8:19). Jesus' success in evangelism did not reside in the sophistication of His marketing method but in who He was. Wisdom does not need the support of marketing and commercials. If we go to Wisdom because of her popularity and because Wisdom is approachable, charming, and seductive, it is not wisdom we will attain. Wisdom is by nature unpopular and difficult to reach.

In other words, says the teacher of Proverbs, "keep your heart with all diligence" (4:23). This advice echoes a previous proverb that urged the student to "keep" Wisdom's sayings "in the midst of your heart" (4:21). The exercise of wisdom is precisely an exercise of our heart, the seat of our most intimate thoughts and intentions. Wisdom will affect our personality deeply; it is a conversion experience. Commenting on this verse, Ellen White refers to the effect of Christ on our life: "When brought into subjection to Christ it must be cleansed by the Spirit from all defilement. This cannot be done without the consent of the individual" (*Seventh-day Adventist Bible Commentary*, 3:1157). The attention to wisdom parallels the attention to our heart; wisdom is thus identified with our heart. Wisdom is not defined here as mere intellectual information, no matter how useful. To have wisdom is to keep control of our heart.

The reason is that from the heart come "the springs of life" (4:23, NASB), just as Wisdom is "the tree of life" (3:18). Our life depends then on what is happening in the secrecy of our heart, how in our most intimate thoughts and sentiments we respond to Wisdom. There is no room here for lies and hypocrisy (4:24). Our words and our appearance are in tune with our inner thoughts. We are not torn between two ways. There is only one way (4:25–27).

Emotional education

The first application of wisdom concerns our emotional life (5:1–2) and will invade our privacy—the place we think of as our own personal domain only, and not another's business. Solomon warns his son against the temptation of adultery. His first argument is the deception and the lies associated with that illusion of love. It is a bittersweet experience. What appears to be like "honey" and "smoother than oil" reveals itself in the end as "bitter as wormwood" (5:3; cf. Deut. 29:18). This liaison is comparable to "a two-edged sword" (5:4), which means that it has a double effect, dividing the personality, "soul and spirit" (Heb. 4:12), and producing some kind of schizophrenia. She claims to walk on the paths of life but goes to death without knowing it (5:6).[1]

The second argument provides the son with specific guidelines to resist this temptation. Solomon's basic advice is to flee far away from that woman and never come close to her (5:8). The best way to resist temptation is not to simply say no. It is more radical; it is to flee, and far away, too. This was Joseph's reaction (Gen. 39:12) with his master's wife. If you do not flee, you will be lost in scandal. All kinds of people, including your personal enemy, "the cruel one" (5:9), but also strangers and even foreigners (5:10), will take advantage of that situation and will plunder you (5:11). You will then bitterly regret having disobeyed your teachers and having ignored instruction (5:12–14). Better to miss the pleasure of one instant than to suffer the desolation of a whole life.

The best defense against the temptation of adultery is your own wife. The metaphor of the well suggests inappropriate and illicit behavior (Gen. 21:25; 26:15). In addition, the comparison to water conveys the promise of life (Jer. 2:13; Rev. 22:17). On one hand, the wise man warns of the forbidden nature of adultery; on the other, he underlines the prospect of life associated with faithfulness. The next point refers

---

1. The verbs translated in the second person masculine singular (NKJV) should rather be translated in the third feminine singular (most translations: ESV, JPS, NIV). In Hebrew the form (2ms and 3fs) is the same.

again to the duty of memory. She is "the wife of your youth" (5:18). You share a common past. To forget her is to deny your past and therefore a part of yourself. To the duty of memory is added the obligation not only to make her happy, have her "be blessed" (5:18a), but also to "rejoice" with her (5:18b–19). Erotic and sensual enjoyment has its place here. Significantly, the Song of Songs uses the same metaphorical language in the same context of love (Song 4:15).

The wise one concludes his plea with a rhetorical question, in order to show that falling into this sin would be absurd (5:20).

The ways of man

The next section (5:21–6:19) will consider in a more general manner the behavior of men and women before the Lord.

The Wicked Man (5:21–23; 6:12–19). The sinner is revealed as a sinner, not only because God has followed all his moves (5:21) but also because his sins will ultimately trap him (5:22). There is an immanent as well as a transcendent judgment. The sinner is punished in his life by his own actions but also beyond this life by God Himself. The wicked will die not just because he is human, like the righteous, but because he ignored God's instruction and went astray (5:23). Our passage here refers to the second death (Rev. 21:8).

The two lists of seven sins (6:12–19) are not intended to be comprehensive. The lists are symbolic, as is the number seven. The number seven and the systematic references to the body parts (mouth, eyes, feet, fingers, and heart in the first list and look, tongue, hands, heart, and feet in the second) suggest the whole body. The idea is that the sinner is totally committed to sin. The sentence that condemns these sins implies death (6:15) and divine reprobation (6:16). Both sentences are included in the first judgment (5:23). The style of the phrase "he shall be broken without remedy" (6:15), which uses the grammatical form of the divine passive ("shall be broken"), means that God is the subject of the verb. God is the direct agent of the destructive judgment. God is the One who will finalize our destiny, precisely because all the ways of man are "before the eyes of the Lord" (5:21). The intention of this discourse is again to make us fully aware of God's omnipresence, and it encourages us to live a holy life, totally committed to God.

The Pledge (6:1–5). This case seems to be out of place here in connection to Solomon's call for a holy life. Yet the example of the pledge belongs paradoxically to the same lesson. Indeed, the point of this passage is to discourage unreasonable zeal. Before we commit ourselves to a good deed, in this instance to "become surety for your friend" (6:1), we have to make sure that we can afford it. Otherwise we will trap ourselves (6:2).

Solomon gave the same advice in his other book: "Do not be overly righteous, nor be overly wise: why should you destroy yourself" (Eccles. 7:16). The apostle Paul resonates with this counsel: "I want you to be wise about what is good, and innocent about what is evil" (Rom. 16:19, NIV). The wise one of the book of Proverbs says the same thing. While he is categorically opposed in regard to evil, and does not tolerate half measures on this matter, he is more nuanced when he refers to good actions. Besides the case of the pledge, other examples come to mind, such as the charitable person who gives too much money to the poor, who will then exploit him; or the generous teacher who gives only good grades and then becomes a prisoner of the grade inflation that he himself has created.

If by chance we make this kind of mistake, it is important that we free ourselves and change the rules of the game. Solomon insists vehemently that we should not let matters get out of hand. We should take the initiative: "go and humble yourself" (6:3). Otherwise, warns the wise one, we will become prisoner of a system that we have created, regardless of our best intentions, and the good will turn into evil for everyone involved.

The Ant (6:6–11). On the other hand, urges Solomon, consider the ant and follow her model. Solomon's appeal, "*go [lekh] to the ant*" (6:6), echoes his precedent invitation to "*go [lekh] and humble yourself*" (6:3). Referring to the model of the ant, Solomon lays down three fundamental principles. First, do it by yourself. Just as the ant, which has "no captain, overseer or ruler" (6:7) and decides by herself to work, so you do not need directions and orders. If you do the right thing because you are commanded to do so, you will do it, not because it is good, but because you are afraid for your business or your advancement, or because it is your legal obligation, just as when we pay taxes. Second, learn to anticipate the future. Just as the ant saves in the summer in order to supply for the rigor and the misery of the winter, learn to foresee the potential crisis and prepare for it. This wisdom is perfectly exemplified by Joseph, who saved the grain during the seven good years in preparation of the following seven years of hunger (Gen. 41:34–36). The wisdom of anticipating the future and weighing the consequences of one's actions is often emphasized in biblical wisdom as an incentive for making the right choice (4:9–11). The criterion for true wisdom is a perspective on the future. "No scheme of business or plan of life can be sound or complete that embraces only the brief years of this present life and no provision for the unending future" (Ellen G. White, *Education,* 145). The future becomes, then, the measuring rod to test and evaluate the situation. Third, the wise one of Proverbs deplores the passivity of the sluggard; he, instead, calls for action.

The word *little* occurs three times in the same line (6:10) as a kind of warning. The sin of the sluggard appears to be just "a little" sin, not important or harmful. Then, because it is deemed as "little," we do not take it seriously, and keep doing it, without awareness of the danger. The consequence for this behavior is catastrophic. Poverty will surprise us like a robber.

The parable of *The Little Prince* by the French writer Antoine de Saint-Exupéry conveys the same lesson. The little prince did not care about the "little" grass growing in his garden. One day he woke up and the "little" plants had become huge baobabs. It was too late, then, to control the situation. The garden was lost.

The parallel between the sluggard and the wicked man presents an interesting irony. Both have a problem with their sleep. While the wicked man lost his sleep in his eagerness to harm his neighbor, the sluggard lost himself in his sleep for lack of eagerness.

CHAPTER 3

Playing With Fire

What is striking and may surprise the reader is the fact that the wise man of Proverbs seems to repeat himself. Again he emphasizes the importance of the Law, and again he denounces the evil of the strange woman, who is more threatening and fateful than ever. This repetition is a part of his teaching method. The teacher wants to make sure that his student will hear him, if not the first time, then perhaps the second. To teach is to repeat. The ancient teachers of the rabbinic schools were called the *Tannaim,* which means "those who repeat." They were not indeed just repeating the lessons they had learned from their teachers; they also repeated the same lessons over and over until their students had well assimilated the material. It was not, however, a mechanical repetition of the same words. Often, the teacher returned to the same message and expanded it and intensified it.

The Law

The pedagogical method of repetition is already obvious in the teacher's introduction to the Law. Both the father and the mother will join their forces in that enterprise, saying the same thing with their own voice and intonation and with their own emphasis. The parallelism repeats and intensifies the lesson. The idea of "bind them around your heart" is intensified and expanded in the next line, which is: "tie them around the neck" (6:21). The law is first received and assimilated in the heart, the seat of our thoughts and our intimate sentiments, and from there moves to the neck, whose function is to orient the direction one is to take. This Law has many qualities.

Continuity. It is not enough to recognize the value of the Law and make the decision to do the right thing. Obedience has to be repeated and should be lasting; hence the use of the adverb "continually" (6:21). The Hebrew word *tamid* (translated here "continually") refers to the continual fire that is supposed to burn on the altar without interruption (Num. 4:16; Dan. 11:31). This lasting quality of faithfulness to the Law reappears in its functions. The Law is always present also. Our faithfulness to the Law responds to the faithfulness of the Law toward us. The Law will "keep" us even when we are asleep (6:22). The idea is that our obedience to the Law has prevented us from potential bad actions, and thus allowed us to sleep in good conscience.

Yet this protection is not just the result of our behavior. Obedience is an act of faith. In obeying God, we have entrusted God with our life. He is the One who is in control of our life. The Law suggests a passive quality on our part. We let God do it for us. In addition, the Law has an active quality; the Law will also converse with us, inspire us, guide us, and enrich our life. This description of Law suggests that the Law is more than a dead set of rules and implies a continuous relationship with a person who is continually present.

Light. From the association of the ideas of "sleep" and "awake" the poet of Proverbs moves naturally to the idea of "light." This connection between the light and the Law occurs often in the Scriptures. The connection is already suggested in the etymological relation between the word *Torah* ("Law") and *'or* ("light"). Thus in his praising of the Law, the author of the Psalms compares it to "a light to my path" (Ps. 119:105). The Law functions like a lamp that enlightens my path and helps me recognize where I am and thus helps orient my walking (Ps. 19:8). This association with the light elevates the Law to a divine status.

God is indeed often compared to the light (2 Sam. 22:29; Ps. 36:9; Mic. 7:8; Isa. 60:20). The reason for this identification is that the Law is given by God and is an expression of His character. Jesus is often identified with the light (John 1:4; 8:12; 9:5).

Life. The association of light and life is also well attested in Hebrew tradition (Job 3:20; 33:30; Ps. 49:19). The psalmist asks God that he "may walk before God in the light of life" (Ps. 56:13, NIV). Jesus is described as "life, and the life was the light of men" (John 1:4). Jesus promises His disciples that "whoever follows [Him] will never walk in darkness, but will have the light of life" (John 8:12, NIV). In the book of Revelation, the tree of life is associated with the light provided by God, evoking the *menorah,* the candelabra of the temple (Rev. 22:3–5). The word *life* is a key word in this passage (6:23, 26; 7:2). Each occurrence of the word *life* conveys one particular lesson.

The first occurrence of that word reminds us that the Law is "the way of life" (6:23). The Law concerns, then, the way we live, and should therefore affect all our choices and all our actions. The immediate application of this principle is the evil woman (6:24) from whom the Law will "keep" us (6:24). This woman is dangerous because she gives the impression that she will give life. She flatters and makes you believe that you are handsome and important and that you are the seducer, while she is really the "seductress" (6:24). She is beautiful and makes your heart beat faster, while her beauty is just a manipulation of her "eyelids" (6:25). She is cheap, just "a crust of bread" (cf. JPS), and makes you believe that you are taking advantage of her (6:26) when you are in fact her victim. She is the one who will take advantage of your "precious life" (6:26).

This is the second use of the word *life.* To prove his point, the wise man of Proverbs uses two comparisons. First, he refers to the fire to say that one cannot play with fire without being burned (6:27–29). The unavoidable result is suggested through the literary device of the rhetorical question (cf. Amos 3:3–8). Second, he refers to the case of the thief. Even if the thief steals because he is hungry, he is still penalized and will have to "restore sevenfold" (6:31). But the one who commits adultery will be penalized even more.

The wise man suggests that there is a fundamental difference between the two cases. While the former can compensate the owner for his theft of an object or an animal (see Exod. 22:1–4), the latter cannot, for his action concerns humans. The husband "will not accept any compensation" (NIV). While there are possible reparations for stealing, there is none for adultery. Money cannot compensate the husband for the loss of his wife. What the husband has lost has no price. The husband cannot replace it. This is why Mosaic legislation stipulated the death penalty for adultery (Lev. 20:10), although one is not sure to what extent this sentence was really applied in ancient Israelite society. Paradoxically, in our societies, stealing will be punished while adultery will be smiled at. In the context of Proverbs, the ancient lesson remains, however: adultery will cost the life of the adulterer.

It is very possible that the case of adultery is used in the rhetorical argumentation of Proverbs to illustrate the more general problem of sin. In that perspective the adulterous/wicked/evil woman may represent Evil just as the good woman represents Wisdom. The conclusion of the speech seems to support this interpretation: "My son, keep . . . my commands and live" (7:1–2). This third and last reference to life echoes, as an inclusio, the introduction where the same phrase, "my son, keep your father's command" (6:20) is used; it is there also associated with the words *Law* (*torah*) and *heart* in connection with the same imagery of binding (6:21).

This echo is, however, slightly nuanced and contrasted. The binding is now applied to the fingers, and the heart is now compared to a tablet on which the son has to write the Law (7:3). The fingers symbolize the action, and the heart symbolizes the thinking. The lesson is that the Law does not just concern our concrete life, what we do; it has also to invade the intimacy of our thoughts and motivations, as in the very terms of the "new covenant," as stipulated by the prophet Jeremiah: "This is the covenant that I will make with the house of Israel after those days, says the LORD: I will put My law in their minds, and write it on their hearts; and I will be their God, and they shall be My people" (Jer. 31:33).

As for the "apple of your eye" (7:2), which qualifies the Law to connote the idea of something precious, it is associated with the capacity to see, somehow responding to the association of light (6:23) and "precious life" (6:26). The adulteress, the wicked woman who brings death (6:26, 32), stands in contrast to Wisdom, which generates life (7:2) and is called "my sister" (7:4), a denomination that characterizes the good loving wife (Song 5:1). This antithesis between the two women would, then, confirm the spiritual identification of the adulteress as the personification of sin and evil, just as the good woman would personify faithfulness to the Law of God, language that belongs to the classic conjugal metaphor of the Scriptures.

The harlot

The next scene is an object lesson. The wise man presents himself as a witness who catches the harlot and her victim by surprise. The testimony of the wise man is all the more objective and lucid, as he is in the position of observing without being seen (7:6). The story begins and ends with the same scene of the simple young man on his way to the harlot (7:8–9 and 7:22–23). Between these two moves by the young man, which mark the beginning and the end of his walk, the harlot's strategy is unveiled (7:10–21).

The Beginning of the Journey. The potential victim of the harlot is spotted among the young and the naïve (7:7). The son will easily recognize himself here. There is nothing wrong with being young and naïve, and not all the young and naïve will fall into the trap of the harlot. One of them, however, has something special that is not found among the other young and naïve men: he is "devoid of understanding" (7:7). In Hebrew the phrase reads literally "devoid of heart." While in his preceding discourse the wise man recommended that his son use his heart, this naïve young man has no heart to use. He has lost his mind and does not think.

At first it seems that the young man is just accidentally passing by (7:8a). Yet the next verb clearly suggests that he knows where he is going: he walks to the house of the harlot (7:8b). What may have appeared to be just chance was in fact premeditated. The young man knew where this harlot lived, and he had already imagined and planned his journey to her. Amazingly, he can even find his way in the dark (7:9). To evoke the "dark," the Hebrew text refers to "the apple of the eye of the night" (literal translation). At the same time, the Hebrew poet points back to the "apple of the eye" of the law (7:2). Ironically, what was precious for the wise son has become a stumbling block for the fool.

The Harlot's Moves. Apparently, the harlot had already noticed him, since she knows where he is. The word *hinneh,* "there," suggests her sudden appearance; and the Hebrew verb *qr'* (translated "met") occurs often in the context of war (Gen. 14:17; Josh. 11:20), implying that she comes *aggressively* in his direction. These details indicate that the harlot has in fact prepared her moves well in advance, in contrast to the young man, who is described as being totally vulnerable and easy prey. While she has a "crafty heart" (7:10), he has no heart at all (7:7). While she is self-confident, "loud and defiant" (7:11, NIV), he is silent and never speaks. It is noteworthy that she is the only one who talks. The poor young man has nothing to say and is overwhelmed by her powerful presence. While she knows her way around, "lurking at every corner" (7:12), he does not seem to know where he is going. Strangely, and contrary to normal practice, she is the one who takes the initiative. She is the one who seeks him and finds him (7:15). She is the one who invites and proposes (7:18). And lastly, she is the one who offers three good reasons to convince the young man.

The first reason is religion. She has done all her pious duties. She has offered her peace sacrifices, and she has paid her vows (7:14). Even her language that depicts her iniquity is religious. When she claims to "diligently . . . seek" (7:15), she uses a Hebrew verb *shkhr* that is often used to refer to the seeking of God (Gen. 19:27; Job 8:5; Ps. 63:2). The word will be retained in Jewish liturgy (Talmud, *Ber* 26b) to designate the first prayer of the day, the morning prayer, the *shakharit*. The woman has then ~~turned her iniquity into a devotional, a time of worship.~~ She has ~~a good conscience before God,~~ and therefore they can go ahead together. ~~God is with them and will bless their lo~~ve. Note that she is ~~not disconnecting religion from~~ her life. On the contrary, sh~~e is includ-~~ ~~ing God in her plan.~~

This is the first deception, to believe and m~~ake believe that God is~~ ~~with us while we are committing our iniquity.~~ Ironically and dangerously, this was the claim of the Wehrmacht soldiers in World War II, who engraved this motto on their belt: *"Gott mit uns"* ("God with us"). ~~When we think God is with us while committing iniquity, we will do~~ ~~it with religious zeal and fanaticism.~~ We will think that w~~e kill with~~ ~~God's approval,~~ and ultimately that we will ~~kill~~ *for* ~~God.~~ On a more banal level, when we turn our personal, human opinions and our own choices into a religious affair, we are elevating ourselves to divine status. We proceed like the builders of Babel, who wanted to go up to the "door of God" and thus take His place (Gen. 11:4). The Bible calls this sin idolatry, for we have identified God with ourselves, and we have created God in our image.

The second reason is ~~pleasure~~. Once the religious obstacle has been taken away, the woman can be more direct and openly describes the environment of their encounter. She points very suggestively to the bed where their love will take place. All senses are alerted. The tapestry and the colored coverings (7:16) and the rich perfumes (7:17) provide visual and fragrant support to her evocation. Once the environment is set up, she is then explicit about the intensity of their activities, which will be full until the morning (7:18). The word *love* is repeated twice (7:18). This is the first time that the first-person plural is used: "let us," which is also used twice in the same verse. So far she was referring only to the first or the second person.

The third reason is security. The absence of her husband is the

for Woman

assurance that there is no risk. Her husband will be far away[1] on "a long journey" (7:19), which is evidenced by the bag of money he has taken with him. He has gone away on important business. The man she is referring to may not even be her husband. The Hebrew text means literally, "the man is not in his house," which suggests that the woman does not consider him as her husband, or that she simply lives with him in his house. This way of qualifying her husband is also another manner of reaching out to the young man. She belongs to no one and is therefore available for him.

The fact that she specifies the moment of his return as the "full moon" (7:20, NIV) suggests that she has more in view than a simple night. At the same time, it is ironic that religious duty should put an end to their adultery, as it was "religious" duty that first allowed it. For the woman, religion is just empty rituals and traditions. It is a cultural religion. She never refers to God. Likewise, we may keep the Sabbath and pay our tithes and regularly attend our religious services, and yet be involved in iniquity, live outside of marriage with someone, or entertain an adulterous relationship. We may be very pious and zealous in our religious acts and yet live an immoral life: stealing, lying, committing adultery, abusing our spouse, and even murdering.

The sad paradox is that often the most religiously zealous are also the most unethical people. Religion can function as a mask to hide our weakness or as a compensation for our iniquity.

The End of the Journey. The adverb *immediately* suggests the promptness of the young man's response to the charm of the woman. The verb describing his move, "he went" (7:22), suggests a determined pace, which contrasts with the hesitant pace he had in the beginning of his journey, when "he took the path" (7:8). Before, he was just walking; now he goes. The tragic irony is that the end of his journey corresponds also to the end of his life. The young playboy, who thought of himself as handsome, smart, a bon vivant, is in fact a stupid ox who "goes to the slaughter"; a fool who goes to the stocks to be beaten (7:22); or a

---

1. The Hebrew has *merakhoq,* which means "far away" (Gen. 22:4; 2 Kings 2:7; Isa. 59:14).

ridiculous little bird that "hastens to the snare" (7:23). Little does he know that all this adventure will cost him his life (7:23b).

This truth unveils, at last, the message hidden under this sordid affair: sin leads to death. This is the ultimate lesson that should be retained: flirting with the adulterous woman "is a highway to the grave, leading down to the chambers of death" (7:27, NIV).

CHAPTER 4

The Urgency of Wisdom

There is a story about a man who woke up one morning and looked around. He heard the bad news of the streets near and far. The man felt hopeless. He decided, then, to warn the world. He went to the middle of his town and stood up on the highest podium and started to shout his story. Every morning he came to the same place to tell the same story. It was a beautiful story about flowing rivers, colorful flowers, and buzzing butterflies, a story of peace, of love and life—a story of rainbows and stars. It was a story of nostalgia, nice memories, a story that called for change.

In the beginning, many people came. They were intrigued by this strange man and his strange story. Yet, as days passed, fewer and fewer people came. One morning, as the man was shouting his same strange and beautiful story, and his same dramatic call for change, he felt someone pulling his coat. A child, the only human left in the place, warned him: "Look, you are alone in the place, no one is listening to you; it does not make sense to shout every morning. Why do you keep telling that story? You will not change the world." The man looked around, and indeed the place was deserted. He thought for a moment and then he answered. "I will keep shouting my story; for before I told the story to change the world. Now, I will tell the story so that the world does not change me."

This parable accounts for the hopeless condition of the world and the desperate need to shout about the need for change. Against the prospect of death associated with the foolish woman (7:27), we urgently need to hear the desperate cries of Wisdom (8:1–21). We need to realize that Wisdom is not just an option among others. Wisdom is not simply an interesting idea or a nice insight. We need to understand that Wisdom is the beginning of everything, the only way out (8:22–36). We need to hear her call and respond; for it is not just a charming song we will enjoy and then forget about and go to other activities. Wisdom will shake us and propel us on another path. Wisdom will oblige us to choose between life with her (9:1–12) and death with Folly (9:13–18).

The universality of wisdom

Wisdom has to shout (8:1). There is much noise all around us. We are busy with so many "important" activities and are so fully entertained that we hardly hear the voice of Wisdom. There are so many competitive claims for our attention that it has become difficult, if not impossible, to hear her voice. And yet everyone needs to hear her story, which contains a universal message.

The wisdom we are talking about here is not just a new product from an exotic place, not just the "in" idea of the moment. This Wisdom is to be heard everywhere at all times. Wisdom must take "her stand on the top of the high hill" (8:2a) in order that everyone may see her, just like the light Jesus urged to be set out where it can be seen. For it is not reasonable to "light a lamp and put it under a basket, but on a lampstand, and it gives light to all who are in the house" (Matt. 5:15). Wisdom must be encountered everywhere: "beside the way" (8:2b) where people walk back and forth, heading to their jobs or simply having a promenade; "where the paths meet" (8:2c), at the crossroads where people travel from many directions, for business or for pleasure; "by the gates" (8:3), where the city is governed. Wisdom must reach all humanity (8:4), including the "simple ones" (8:5) and the "fools" (8:5).

The reason why wisdom has to be heard is its content. Wisdom counts two major qualities. The first characteristic of wisdom is that it speaks truth (8:7). Wisdom will not deceive us. Wisdom will not speak according to our wishes, but it will reveal the true nature of things. With wisdom we will know who we really are, and we will also learn the right path to take. The apostle Paul warns us against the tendency to hear only what fits the best with our wishes and our opinions: "For the time will come when they will not endure sound doctrine, but according to their own desires, because they have itching ears, they will heap up for themselves teachers; and they will turn their ears away from the truth, and be turned aside to fables" (2 Tim. 4:3–4). Wisdom will give us the courage and the lucidity to see and confront the reality.

This is why Jesus relates truth to the way of holiness: "Sanctify them by Your truth" (John 17:17). Truth is thus connected to God Himself. Jesus said: "I am . . . the truth" (John 14:6). No one has the absolute truth; as the Arab poet Khalil Gibran put it, "Say not, 'I have found the truth,' but rather, 'I have found a truth.'" The point is not that the truth does not exist, but that my view is only *a* truth among others. Only God is *the* truth. And this is what makes the truth universal. The truth has to be universal, truth for all, or it is not the truth.

The second characteristic of wisdom is that, although it is available to anyone and is real, it is not cheap and ordinary. Wisdom is even more precious than gold, silver, and rubies (8:10–11; cf. 8:18–19, 21). In fact, wisdom is so precious that its value transcends all our common desires (8:11). Wisdom will surprise us with her beauty. There is also an element of faith in the choice of wisdom. At first wisdom will look simplistic and plain; it will even disturb us. Yet it is profound and wonderful. Wisdom contains the truth about us. This was the prayer of Christian poet Michel Quoist: "O God give me the grace to discover and to live what you dreamed about me."[1]

Wisdom is not just for the simpleton or for the fool, although the fool

---

1. Translated from French by the author, from Michel Quoist, *Prières* (Ivry-sur-Seine: Editions de l'Atelier, 2003), 114.

47

needs wisdom the most. Ironically, wisdom is the most needed by those who think they are wise, that is, the proud and the arrogant (8:13). Wisdom is required in the highest ranks of government. At this level, foolishness is dangerous because it will involve more than the mere fool himself.

The primacy of wisdom

The poet of Proverbs reaches now the climax in his apology of wisdom. The highest superlative is found to qualify Wisdom. She is closely related to God as the Creator. She is "the beginning of His way" (8:22). The word for "beginning" is *bere'shit,* and that belongs specifically to the divine creation (Gen. 1:1). It has an absolute sense, referring to the totality of the universe ("heavens and earth"), that is, the absolute creation of the universe ("heavens and earth"). This passage has often been applied to the second person of the Trinity (see, for example, *Patriarchs and Prophets,* 34) in order to emphasize His involvement in the act of creation: "All things were made through Him, and without Him nothing was made that was made" (John 1:2; cf. Col. 1:16).[2] The word *beginning* does not imply, however, that this divine Wisdom (alias Jesus Christ) had a beginning, and that He had been created then. The Hebrew verb *qnh,* translated "possessed" (8:22), is the same as the one referring to the "birth" of Eve's firstborn, which was interpreted by Eve as the extraordinary birth of YHWH, the Lord, as the following literal translation suggests: "I have gotten [*qnh*] . . . the LORD" (Gen. 4:1). The Hebrew syntax indeed gives "the LORD" as the direct complement object of the verb *qnh.* Eve's exclamation did not imply that she had created YHWH but that she thought YHWH had incarnated Himself in this first human newborn.[3] The verb *qnh* means generally "to acquire," "to possess," and very rarely has the sense of "create."[4]

To say that God "possessed" (*qnh*) wisdom at the "beginning"

---

2. See also ancient rabbinic interpretation that identifies Wisdom in this passage with the Torah, the Law of God, through which God created the world (*Genesis Rabbah* 1:6).

3. See J. Doukhan, *On the Way to Emmaus: Five Major Messianic Prophecies Explained* (Clarksville, MD: Messianic Jewish Publishers, 2012), 22; cf. Ellen G. White, *The Desire of Ages,* 31.

4. Out of the eighty-four occurrences of the verb, only six allow the meaning of "create."

(*bere'shit*) of His way in the work of the creation of the universe is to suggest that God had wisdom since the very beginning of the creative operation. This does not mean that wisdom was created at that moment. We have already encountered the same idea earlier: "The LORD by wisdom founded the earth; by understanding He established the heavens" (3:19). It is this primacy of wisdom in creation that retains the attention of the poet. The literary structure of the Genesis Creation story (Gen. 1:1–2:4a) is reflected throughout the poem. Wisdom is present for any creation and at every step. Wisdom is involved in the creation of the three elements of the created world ("heavens," "water," and "earth"), a series that is repeated twice, in parallel to the Genesis Creation story:

- In the beginning (*re'shit*), heavens and earth (8:22//Gen. 1:1–2)
- heavens (8:23//Gen. 1:3–8)
- water (8:24//Gen. 1:9)
- earth (8:25–26//Gen. 1:10–13)
- heavens (8:27//Gen. 1:14–19)
- water (8:28–29a//Gen. 1:20–23)
- earth (8:29b–31a//Gen. 1:24–31)
- heavens and earth implied (8:31b//Gen. 2:1–4)

The rhythm of seven that constitutes the structure of the Genesis Creation story reappears in the wisdom poem, marking the seven exclamations of Wisdom speaking in the first person: "I have been established" (8:23), "I was brought forth" (8:24), "I was brought forth" (8:25), "I was there" (8:27), "I was beside Him" (8:30a), "I was daily His delight" (8:30b), "my delight was with the sons of men" (8:31).

The purpose of the beautiful and symmetrical architecture of the poem is again to emphasize the primacy of Wisdom. This exaltation of Wisdom is reinforced by her intimacy with the divine. Wisdom is in fact identified with God. The divine identity of Wisdom is indicated not only through her essential connection with the Lord (8:22), and through her systematic association with Him in the course of the creative operation (8:23–30), but it is suggested also through the use of the technical expression *'ehyeh,* "I was" (8:30), which characterizes YHWH (see Exod. 3:14).

The poem ends on a different note. While the whole text draws attention to the grandeur and transcendence of wisdom, thus inspiring reverence, the conclusion insists on her proximity to humans: "My delight was with the sons of men" (8:31). It is noteworthy that this confession occurs at the seventh step, which parallels the Sabbath in the Genesis Creation story, the only day of the Creation week when God enjoys fully the company of humans (Gen. 2:2–3).

The call of Wisdom is rooted in this tension of reverence and joy. If Wisdom is so powerful and so loving, the only conclusion possible is to take her words seriously, to listen to her (8:32–34a), to seek for her with passion, attention, and perseverance (8:34b), and then respond to her call. Again the two ways are displayed. Either we embrace Wisdom, and then we will find life and grace from the Lord (8:35), or we embrace folly, and then we will lose our life (8:36).

The way of wisdom

The Wisdom "master craftsman" (8:30) who created the world in seven days is the same who "has hewn out her seven pillars" (9:1). The image reminds us of the ancient Egyptian temples with their pillars, representing the "Island of Creation," whose function was to trigger and nurture the nostalgia of that "Island of Creation," suggesting a return to that idyllic time. Wisdom thus extends an invitation to return to the time of Creation, to enjoy again the goodness of the pre-fallen world.

This metaphor of the ultimate banquet will often be used in the Scriptures to illustrate the eschatological hope. David elaborates on that motif: "You prepare a table. . . . You anoint my head with oil; my cup runs over. Surely goodness and mercy shall follow me all the days of my life; and I will dwell in the house of the Lord forever" (Ps.

23:5–6). Jesus' parable of the wedding feast (Matt. 22:1–14; cf. Luke 14:15–24) echoes many elements of that banquet of Wisdom. At that time, the servants are sent all over to invite people to the festive meal, and the response of the guests is mixed. Likewise, the book of Revelation speaks about the eschatological banquet that will welcome the saints with rejoicing (Rev. 19:7–9).

In our passage the invitation of Wisdom is extended to two categories of persons, the "simple," or the one "who lacks understanding" (9:4), and the "scoffer," or the "wicked" (9:7). Whereas the scoffer is not open to the criticism and will hate you if you try to challenge him (9:7–8), the wise will love you for it (9:8b).

What characterizes the wise is not so much that he is wise but that he feels the need to be wise. Only the "wise," then, will feel the need to respond, and will therefore become wiser (9:9). The unjust will be stuck in his wickedness; the righteous will blossom in his righteousness (Rev. 22:11). Wisdom apart from God is impossible. The wise reasserts his affirmation with which he began: "The fear of the LORD is the beginning of wisdom" (9:10; cf. 1:7). Secular and atheistic ethics and wisdom lead nowhere. Thinking that we can reach wisdom by ourselves, outside of the realm of divine revelation, is an illusion.

The poetic meditation on Wisdom in creation explains why. This is a simple biological truth: God, being the Creator, is the Source of life (9:11). Everything, then, is in God's hands, everything except the fear of God, which remains in yours. In other words, you are responsible for your destiny: "If you are wise, you are wise for yourself, and if you scoff, you alone will bear it" (9:12).

The way of folly

The other way is described in stark contrast to the way of wisdom. While the first way is represented by a wise woman who provides understanding (9:6), builds her house (9:1), provides festive meals to her guest (9:2, 5), and promises life (9:11)—the second way is represented by a foolish woman in a language reminiscent of adultery. She is "loud" (*homiah*) like the adulteress (9:13; cf. 7:11), doing nothing but seducing the one who is "simple, . . . who lacks understanding" (9:16; 7:6–7; cf. 9:4). She offers "stolen water," alluding to illicit sexual relations (9:17; 5:15–17) and to "bread eaten in secret" (9:17; cf. 7:19–20). Finally, she will lead her guests to "the depths of the grave" (9:18, NLT; cf. 7:27).

CHAPTER 5

Wisdom Is Righteousness

One can be intelligent and smart and yet be a fool and lack wisdom. This paradox has often been observed in our societies. Brilliant and well-educated scholars can live unhealthy and chaotic lives, while simple-minded people with little education can live coherent and healthy existences. Intelligent men are sometimes wicked and hateful while mentally limited people can be kind and loving. Solomon, who was brilliant and well educated, cannot be suspected of anti-intellectualism; yet he deplores this strange contradiction and tries to repair it in this new section (10:1–22:16), a collection of 375 proverbs (the numerical value of the Hebrew name of Solomon), which bears his name in its introduction (10:1).

Solomon's basic thesis is that Wisdom and intelligence cannot be separated from righteousness and spiritual life. To make his point, Solomon uses the Hebrew literary device of setting the two categories in parallel, either in contrasting them in an antithetic manner (A but B), or in comparing them (A better than B). Significantly, the word *tsadiq*, "righteous," is the key word of this section, where it occurs twenty-one times. Contrary to the ideal defended in many of our secular societies, Wisdom and intelligence should be related to holiness and righteousness and should be identified with the fear of God. And contrary to the

53

apologies promoted in many religious circles, religious and holy life should not be dissociated from Wisdom and intelligence. Solomon's purpose is to demonstrate, in fact, that the two categories belong together: Wisdom is righteousness.

Either life or death

Solomon opens his didactic plea with an emotional argument. Wisdom and foolishness are respectively associated with the joy of the father and the sadness of the mother (10:1). Rather than just keeping in mind the rigorous rightness of his father's and mother's arguments, the son will now "feel" them before his actions; he will remember in his heart the joyful face of his father or the sad face of his mother. Even if he does not totally or immediately agree with them, he will act simply out of love for them, because of his relationship with them. The joy of his father and the sadness of his mother will inspire his choices in life. Again the paradigm of the two ways outlined in the book of Deuteronomy is projected, with a perspective of either life or death.

Wickedness Versus Righteousness. The basic principle is first laid down from which all the rest can be derived. On one hand, the many treasures, the wealth accumulated by the wicked, will bring no profit to him, for the wicked will die and will not be saved from death (10:2b). On the other hand, the righteous person who may have nothing will be delivered from death (10:2a). The essential reason for this difference is attributed to the Lord. While the Lord will not allow the righteous to starve and will hear their cry, He will ignore the desires of the wicked (10:3). It is the Lord who "makes one rich" without "sorrow" (10:22). It is the fear of the Lord that "prolongs days" (10:27) and the way of the Lord that provides "strength for the upright" (10:29).

This does not mean, however, that the righteous is passive and just enjoys God's blessings in his or her bed. Precisely because of a personal relationship with the Lord, the righteous entertains a specific work ethic. What has been attributed to the Lord is seen as the direct result of the effort of the righteous and is found on the level of human life.

While righteous people receive words of blessings openly, the wicked covers words of violence that are directed against them (10:6). The memory of the righteous is preserved while the wicked is forgotten (10:7). The wise is open to instructions while the wicked falls (10:8). The one who practices integrity has a secure business, while the one who deceives is ultimately denounced (10:9). The wicked will be the victim of his own fear while the righteous will be reassured (10:24). The wicked will enjoy evil and will therefore no longer be able to discern between good and evil, while the wise will appreciate the value of discernment (10:23). The contribution of the sluggard who does not do his homework and does not prepare himself seriously will be counterproductive (10:26).

All these proverbs, which have here been decoded and paraphrased, substantiate Solomon's observation, namely that we always reap what we sow—good or bad.

The Power of the Tongue. An important place is given to the domain of speech. While the words of the righteous burst out like "a well of life," a notion associated with the Garden of Eden and the eschatological temple (Ezek. 47:1–2; cf. Gen. 2:10), the words of the wicked hide acts of violence (10:11). While the use of many words is associated with sin, the restriction of words is wise (10:19). Solomon refers primarily here to the simple act of being talkative. Words are precious and should therefore be used with care. Those who speak with ease are tempted to enjoy the sound and music of their words instead of paying attention to the content of their discourse and being aware of the person they are speaking to. The result is just a meaningless blather.

While the tongue of the righteous is precious and enriching, the words of the wicked are worthless (10:19–21). While words of hatred trigger strife and tensions, words of love produce forgiveness and repentance (10:12; cf. James 5:20). While the words of the righteous are well received, the speech of the wicked is silenced (10:31–32). Professionals of the word—politicians and also ministers who use the power of words to win their case, to preach and exhort—should meditate on the power of their words. Indeed, the pulpit has often been used to promulgate hatred, and the words that should have pointed to life have often generated violence and death instead.

Words may bring life, but words may also kill. In these days of the Internet, where words are delivered as raw products, without the face of the speaker present, and without the physical presence of the listener, words have become even more dangerous. The problem of our words is that when they are pronounced, we do not control their effect and their interpretation anymore. Another proverb may encapsulate the teaching of the wise on the delicate matter of managing the power of our tongue: "Speech is silver, but silence is gold."

More is less, and less is more

The next section continues with the same contrasting language, but this time the lesson is conveyed through a paradox that surprises and obliges us to combine the opposites. A positive quality may indeed contain its negative evil. Blessing may be the occasion for a curse. On the other hand, having less may be the opportunity to get more. Solomon, who had everything, knows very well that wealth, power, charm, and sovereignty do not come alone and are not the safeguard from misery. In fact, they are often the very cause for stumbling. On the other hand, Solomon had the experience that he was never so wise as when he felt simple and lacking in intelligence (1 Kings 3:7–9).

The first illustration of this paradoxical truth is found in the domain of business. We may become rich with a deceptive scale (11:1), by manipulating the account, or introducing lies in our expense report. But this operation, which is seen only by the Lord, is the implicit affirmation that we dismiss God's presence. On the other hand, if we are honest, knowing that we will lose money, we live according to the principles of faith, "the substance of things hoped for, the evidence of things not seen" (Heb. 11:1). In the latter case, we experience God's proximity, and God fully enjoys it. We live with hope, in the perspective of another kingdom (Heb. 11:1a), and with the conviction that what we do not see is really what matters (Heb. 11:1b). This is the shocking truth that Jesus taught on the mountain: "Blessed are the poor in spirit," meaning those who are not smart, who do not know, and who do not want to know all the tricks to get through the system—for theirs "is the kingdom of heaven" (Matt. 5:3).

Another proverb suggests one of the keys of this principle: "Riches do not profit in the day of wrath" (11:4). The proverb alludes to death. What's the point of striving to be rich if the way we do it would cost our salvation from death? This quick and dishonest gain will not help us in our confrontation with death, while "righteousness delivers from death" (11:4). Comparing Christians to the runners who run "to obtain a perishable crown" (1 Cor. 9:25a), the apostle Paul brings home this point when he urges his disciples to run for "an imperishable crown" (1 Cor. 9:25b). By losing the perishable, we will gain the imperishable. Solomon has observed this truth of gaining through losing already here in our life: "There is one who scatters, yet increases more" (11:24a). On the other hand, the one who amasses riches through deceitfulness will become poor (11:24b). The generous one who gives freely, without exploiting his client, "will be made rich" (11:25). The Hebrew verb is passive, suggesting that the rich owes his wealth to others and not to his own effort. The explanation for this unusual process is given in the next verse; people will bless the one who is generous to them (11:26), and he will get more clients and will then become rich paradoxically because he was not interested in getting rich.

If we think highly of ourselves (11:2a), and thus despise others we consider as inferiors (11:12), we will know the shame of humiliation (11:2a). This is the sign of our lack of wisdom (11:12). But if we are humble and do not exalt ourselves above others, we will be honored, and our wisdom will be praised (11:2b). Jesus recounts a similar scenario in His parable of the guest at the wedding, which He concludes with the same lesson: "Whoever exalts himself will be humbled, and he who humbles himself will be exalted" (Luke 14:11).

This lesson applies even to the domain of cosmetics (11:22). The woman who primps all the time and is eager to promote her beauty will become ridiculous. Again, the desire to be more ends up producing less. The modest woman who does not speak too much and focuses on the value of invisible charm will be noticed. The man who does not boast and humbly hides his works will one day be blessed (Rev. 14:13). The leader who recognizes his limitations and is not afraid to consult his peers will be safe (11:14). The wise man of Proverbs promises an immediate reward "on the earth" to the righteous, who are concerned with the other kingdom. *A fortiori,* the wicked one who is interested only in the immediate result will know the consequence of his acts in this present life (11:31).

Lies, lies, lies

There is a story about a king who needed to appoint a minister of finance. The king thought that such a job needed the expertise of a great liar. The king, then, organized a lying competition. The person who could offer the greatest lie would be nominated. A good number of candidates came, everyone equipped with their best, most unbelievable lie. The selection was difficult, for the liars were all well trained. The king was embarrassed. Suddenly, he spotted one man humbly sitting in the shadow who seemed out of place in the palace. The king asked him whether he had come for the lies competition. "Oh! No!" responded the man. "Never."

"Why?" inquired the king.

The man answered, "I would never pass such an exam. I never lie."

The king smiled and said, "You just won the contest. This is the greatest lie I ever heard."

The punishment of the liar is that he does not know that he lies, for he will lie to himself and ultimately believe in his own lies. He will lose a sense of reality and will not confront that reality in order to change it or improve it. For him, everything is fine, especially in what he does and in what he is. The fool lives in the fairy tale that he has forged for himself.

Wisdom Is Righteousness

The first symptom of this mentality is the incapacity for the fool to accept criticism (12:1; cf. 13:1). The fool likes to believe that he is perfect: "he is right in his own eyes" (12:15). The result of this attitude is that the fool will never be corrected and will deceive himself and others (12:5). The same irony is noted in the poor who pretends to be rich and gets undeserved respect, in contrast to the genuine rich who does not boast of his riches and is therefore despised (12:9). Having without boasting is better than not having with boasting. In fact, boasting is an indication of emptiness.

The true scholar does not need to expose his science; he does not need to constantly remind the people that he is intelligent and has published many books and is the personal friend of great personalities. The true scholar "conceals knowledge" (12:23a; cf. 13:3). The fool, on the other hand, will post a placard with his picture and print a list in bold of his achievements, and will then unknowingly proclaim his foolishness (12:23; cf. 13:3). The tragedy of this foolish attitude is that the fool will just speak about what he did and will never enjoy the fruit of his fake doing. He will not "roast what he took in hunting" (12:27a). The diligent who does not speak about his achievements will benefit from it (12:27b; cf. 13:7).

The wise man knows that lies have corrupted the world. It is through a lie that the devil caused humanity to fall (Gen. 3:1). Lying is the specialty of the devil. As the Gospel of John explains, "There is no truth in him. When he speaks a lie, he speaks from his own resources, for, he is a liar and the father of it" (John 8:44). The problem of lies is so grave that the wise man devotes a whole section to that topic (12:17–22). The wise one observes the devastation of lies, which harm like "a piercing sword" (12:18), and concludes that "lying lips are an abomination to the Lord" (12:22). The only way to counter the lie is not another lie, bigger than the former one; it is the truth. For only the truth can heal the wounded world (12:18). Paradoxically, only the righteous who "hates lying" can beat the deceit of the wicked (13:5–6).

The delay of hope

A reflection on hope is not out of place here, following a warning against dishonesty and lies. The wise knows the mechanism of this iniquity. It is precisely the lack of hope that produces the need to lie and to deceive. It is because we are eager to get an immediate result and do not wish to wait that we resort to lying. This approach goes against the views of biblical wisdom. In that perspective, waiting is an essential part of life with God.

This is the repeated lesson that we hear with the patriarchs—Abraham, Isaac, and Jacob, each of whom had to wait a long time before the fulfillment of the promises. Moses, who gets impatient and wants an immediate solution for his people, has to flee and wait in the desert of Midian for forty years (Exod. 3:1–10; Acts 7:30) before he can save his people. Even Israel had to wait for forty years in the wilderness before entering the Promised Land (Num. 32:13). The author of Proverbs knows that hope implies the pain of this delay. This is why he frames his ethics in an inclusio with this call for hope. He begins with "hope deferred" (Proverbs 13:12) and ends with "desire accomplished" (13:19). Inserted between these two borders are his appeals for instruction and knowledge (13:13–18). The point is that the longing of the soul is nurtured by the wisdom of righteousness and not by the deceit of lies.

Friends and family

Yet we cannot fight alone against the enemy. We need each other in the wrestling that's part of the great controversy. We need the inspiration, the counsel, and the support of our friends and our family. Proverbs begins its recommendation first with friends (13:20–21) and then with family (13:22–25), because we chose our friends but not our family. The wise one warns that the influence of our friends is so powerful that we run the risk of becoming identified with them.

It can work one of two ways. The wisdom of the wise will contaminate you; you will also be wise with the same wisdom (13:20). On the other hand, if you become the "companion" (ro'eh) of fools, you "will be destroyed" (*yero'a*). The two words *companion* and *destroyed* share the same sound *r'*, which means "evil." Like wisdom, evil is contagious. The next verse reinforces the lesson. The word *za'ah,* which was just implicitly heard in the preceding line (13:20b), is now heard explicitly. It is observed that this "evil" (*ra'ah*) runs fast behind the sinner, like the hostile enemy (Gen. 44:4; Amos 1:11), and will catch him very soon: "Evil pursues sinners" (13:21). The idea is that we are in a context of war and hostility. Note that the sinners run; they are always nervous and in a hurry. The wise, on the other hand, "walks" peacefully (13:20). The Hebrew word *shalom,* "peace," is heard in the Hebrew verb *yeshalem* ("repaid").

The next concern relates our duties to the family (13:22–25). We should provide not only the material necessities of our family, food for the present (13:23) and for the future (13:22), but we should also take care of their spiritual needs (13:24–25). The ancient rabbis of the Mishnah insisted on this principle: "If there is no flour (sustenance) there is no Torah; if there is no Torah there is no flour" (*Pirkey Abot* 3:21). The bread on the table and the study of the Bible are both necessary for our survival and our happiness. One duty without the other is inappropriate and even dangerous. To only care about our comfort and our physical urges leads to materialism, selfishness, and crime. To only care about spirituality, prayer, and Bible study leads to fanaticism, disease, and crime. The righteous who thinks right will eat properly (13:25a). The wicked who does not think correctly will not eat properly (13:25b).

CHAPTER 6

When We Build Castles in the Air

The wise man imagines two kinds of masons (14:1). One builds, the other destroys. Yet both have the same intention, which is to build. The difference between the two masons is that the first one possesses the skills and knows how and where to put his hands, while the second one is so clumsy that each of his moves is devastating. Instead of putting the brick on the wall, he knocks down the wall with his own hands. The irony is that the former has really built the house without even being aware of his contribution; as for the latter, not only did he not build anything, he also destroyed what was already there. The irony is that the latter still keeps building with conviction and with all the pretentions of the professional builder who works on a very important construction project; he has all the technical vocabulary, all the sophisticated tools, and all the good gestures. Yet the result is nothing. He built a castle in the air.

Solomon talked about this topic in his other book: "I made my works great, I built myself houses, and planted myself vineyards. . . . Then I looked on all the works that my hands had done and on the labor in which I had toiled; and indeed all was vanity and grasping for the wind" (Eccles. 2:4, 11). The wise man explains that the main reason for this foolishness is that the fool builds alone; he needs no one but himself; he knows it all. The wise man offers the alternative and lays down the foundation of the right and safe architecture. Against the pride and self-sufficiency of the fool, the wise man presents the values of humility and dependence. Against the empty heavens of the anguished fool, the wise man proclaims the reality of the Presence of the Lord and the assurance that He will have the last word.

The fool needs nothing

The first two verbs situate the contrast between the fool and the wise. While the wise "fears," the fool "despises" (14:2). This proverb does not mean that the wise is a coward and the fool is courageous. The fear implied here refers to the awareness of those other than oneself. It means to see the value of the other person. The wise man recognizes the truth of the other and feels in need of it. The fool despises everyone but himself; he thinks that he is rich and has need of nothing (Rev. 3:17a). The result for this attitude of pride is that the fool is like a rod for himself (14:3), and he becomes "wretched, miserable, poor, blind, and naked" (Rev. 3:17b).

The next proverb plays on this image of delusional riches. The manger is empty because there were no oxen to do the labor (14:4). The emptiness of the barn reveals the vanity of the fool's work, "as one who beats the air" (1 Cor. 9:26). The irony is that the fool seems to be interested in wisdom; "he seeks wisdom" (14:6); he participates in all the colloquiums where he gives his enlightened opinion. Yet his agitation around wisdom leads him nowhere. He speaks about wisdom but has no clue what he is talking about. His words sound wise, but this is false wisdom; it is just "deceit" (14:8). The tragedy is that the fool is not aware of his foolishness, and this worsens foolishness (14:9). The fool thinks so ambitiously that he builds a castle; yet his work is crumbling (14:11a). The wise knows modestly that he has just pitched a tent, but it still stands (14:11b).

The conclusion is that what seems right and great to a man may reveal itself as "the way of death" (14:12). It is not what you see, the flashy project that makes the real value of something; it is what you do not see. Laughter may hide sorrow (14:13a), and what appears to be so promising turns out to be a place of mourning (14:13b). The humble tent will last longer than the impressive building. This parable that contrasts the building to the tent may well also contain a subtle allusion to the sanctuary of the desert built under divine control versus the temple built by Solomon (see 2 Sam. 7:2–6). The point is that modest work with God will survive the glorious work of men.

The psychological mechanism of this process is disclosed in the following proverb. The person who loses his mind feeds himself with "his own ways"; in contrast, the "good man" relies on what is above himself (14:14). The character of the wise contrasts sharply, then, with the character of the fool in many respects. While the fool believes "every word" (14:15a) he hears, consults the horoscopes and the psychics, and relies on the virtues of gems and crystals—the wise man fears God and carefully watches his steps (14:15b).

Paradoxically, the fool who mocks the wise for his naïve faith and his childish fears is the one who trembles on Friday the thirteenth and at the view of a black cat. While the fool "rages" and is "quick tempered" (14:16–17) because he relies only on himself and has all the answers, the wise takes his glory from the knowledge he does not have naturally and painfully acquires. The fool tends to despise and oppress those who are poor in his eyes (14:21, 31) because he ignores his Maker (14:31). The fool cannot, therefore, see the value of the one who is not like him. The wise, on the other hand, sees the face of God in the face of his brother, even of his enemy (Gen. 33:10). The reason why the wise is able to see the value of his brother, even if he is "poor," is that the wise knows his Maker and "honors Him" (14:31b), just as Jacob was able to bow before his brother and embrace him because he had just come out from his embrace with the Lord (Gen. 32:22–32).

No wonder, then, that the wise has the capacity to reverse wrath

(15:1) and turn his enemy into a friend. Rabbinic tradition defines the hero in these terms: "Who is a hero? He who turns an enemy into a friend" (*Avot deRabi Nathan* 23). This is what Jesus meant when He called His disciples to love their enemies (Luke 6:27). He did not ask them to love them as enemies. This would be purely hypocritical, unethical, and impossible to achieve. Instead, Jesus meant to engage us in a new relationship with our enemies—we could love them and be loved by them. But this cannot be done without God's grace (see Dan. 1:9).

The presence of the Lord

In chapters 15–16 the reference to "the LORD" (YHWH) reaches its greatest concentration (I counted twenty occurrences). This emphasis in the center of the book of Proverbs should alert us to the essential point of view of the author of Proverbs. It is the presence of the Lord that determines his views on good and evil and, hence, his ethical program. "The eyes of the LORD are in every place, keeping watch on the evil and the good" (15:3). In his other book, Solomon concludes his essay with the same awareness, which he places in the perspective of the eschatological judgment: "God will bring every work into judgment, including every secret thing, whether good or evil" (Eccles. 12:14).

This tight connection between the religious and the ethical domains inspires every aspect of life. It affects the way we speak. Our speech is comparable to "a tree of life," putting us in the context of the Garden of Eden; otherwise, "a deceitful tongue crushes the spirit" (15:4, NLT). The Hebrew word *ruakh,* "spirit," refers to both a spiritual entity, the mind (Josh. 2:11, Ps. 32:2), and "breath" as the principle of life (Ps. 104:29). The point is that spiritual life has a biological effect. It also affects the quality of our worship services and our prayers. Our bad behavior, our lies, our wicked acts nullify our religion by removing its very *raison d'être,* namely God Himself (15:8–9; cf. 15:29). It affects the intimacy of our thinking.

This principle is affirmed theologically: if God is able to pierce the darkness and the emptiness of death, He can all the more penetrate the ripples of our somber hearts (15:11). This is why the way we think and feel has a powerful effect on our physical health: "A merry heart" illuminates our face, but the "sorrow of the heart" impedes our breathing (15:13; cf. 15:30). What is important then is not so much what we have but how we are. It is not what we have on the outside that makes us happy but what we have on the inside. This truth is repeated in this passage of Proverbs with a number of variations: better is little with God than a treasure "with trouble" (15:16); better a meager meal with love than a feast with hatred (15:17; cf. 17:1); better a poor widow than a proud rich person (15:25; cf. 16:19); better a little money with integrity than a bank account with troubles (15:27; cf. 16:8); and, better self-control and mildness than might and power (16:32).

The Sovereignty of the Lord

The most decisive argument for this philosophy of life is that God is the One who conducts the operations and leads them to the end He has in mind. The omnipresence of the Lord guarantees the right outcome. However active and smart we may have been in preparing life goals, God is the One who will ensure their success or failure (16:1). The wise man explores all the facets of this truth and infers the corresponding lessons from it. We should learn to adjust our plans and our desires to God's will. That an idea looks great to us is not enough to make it right. It may well be that this idea hides wrong and wicked intentions, a personal ambition, or a desire for revenge. We must therefore test this idea in the light of God's perspective. We are warned anyway that "the LORD weighs the spirits" (16:2). He knows what is really behind our proposals and plans.

The wise one counsels that we should commit our plans and our works to the Lord (16:3a). If we do so, he promises, God will fulfill them (16:3b). What is extraordinary is that our plans still remain our plans. God does not force us to have His plans. He respects our creative thinking. Yet these plans should be conceived and shaped in tune with the divine worldview. To make sure that they make it to their end, we have to make sure that they participate in the forces of life and not of death.

The wise man suggests the key for this way of life. We simply need to remember that "the Lord has made all [things] for Himself" (16:4). The idea is not that God has created the world and humans for His own interests, as the myths of the ancient Near East taught. God did not create humans to have them serve Him, but on the contrary to serve them and involve them in His glory. God's purpose of creation is the perfect beauty and majesty of heavens and earth, and of human beings, who tell of God's glory (Ps. 19:2; Gen. 1:26; cf. 1 Cor. 11:7). God's purpose for creation after the Fall is to bring all the creation back to its original status, which was God's glory. Our purpose in life should be to join forces with God and participate in that restoration of God's glory. "Therefore," implores Paul, "whether you eat or drink, or whatever you do, do all to the glory of God" (1 Cor. 10:31).

In response, God assures us that He will produce *shalom* even with our enemies (16:7). He is the One who will produce the miracle of turning our enemies into friends and do so in such a way that His kingdom may be sensed even here on earth and His will be done (Matt. 6:10). The wise man promises that whatever dreams a person may entertain, the Lord will guide and strengthen his steps so that his dreams may take place (16:9). The wise man denounces, however, the abuse of power that often tempts leaders. The syntax of the verbs (jussive form) suggests that the author of Proverbs does not describe here the actual king but the ideal one, how the king should be or not be. The future king should not think that God will bless all his plans, even if they are perverse, simply because he is the king. Power does not us give the right to deceive (16:11) and "commit wickedness" (16:12). The fact that we can do something does not mean that we are allowed to do it. The purpose of power is not to do whatever we want but to do whatever is right: "a throne is established by righteousness" (16:12). The king's power is therefore submitted to the standards of righteousness. The value of this truth is not just affirmed dogmatically. The king should not do righteousness just because it is righteousness, but because he likes righteousness (16:13). Our commitment to righteousness should not derive from a legalistic standpoint but blossom out of love. Thus, our message about righteousness should radiate the positive promise of the vitality, the joy, and the beauty of life instead of carrying the negative threat of sadness and death (16:15).

In that enterprise, the search for wisdom is vital. Rather than look for the immediate and visible reward of wealth, the king should choose wisdom and avoid evil (16:16–17). It is not enough to be right and claim proudly to have the truth; we should communicate our truth with humility (16:18–19) and with the awareness that we are still in need of God's wisdom (16:20). Also, the rightness of the Truth we proclaim does not suffice to make us right in the eyes of those we teach; we have to carefully weigh our words and make our speech pleasant (16:21, 24) and not arrogant, so that our truth may be well received, stimulate learning (16:21), and generate a positive response (16:22a). Otherwise the teaching will be counterproductive and will promote folly (16:22b).

Therefore, the wise man must be teachable and add "learning to his lips" (16:23). The rightness and the beauty of our words are not enough to make us good teachers; we must still remain good students. For the honorable position of teaching may give us the illusion that we have nothing to learn anymore. Whereas the painful assignment of learning obliges us all the time to realize that we need to learn. The more we learn, the more we discover that we need to learn. Indeed, the wise man says that we should not trust our judgment; for we may sometimes have the impression, or even the profound conviction, that our way is right, but in the end we were wrong (16:25). We have been so convinced about the rightness of our position that we have not listened to anyone before. We are therefore to blame, and not God. Although God controls the course of events, we remain free and are fully responsible for their outcome. Our evil actions will generate evil (16:26–30).

The wise man also encourages his student to be respectful to the old teacher. For his great age, rather than being a handicap, is really the reason for his "glory" (16:31a), especially if the old person is "found in the way of righteousness" (16:31b). In other words, the fact that the man is old should not justify our contempt; instead it should encourage our respect. Yet old age is not necessarily a guarantee of wisdom or a sure barrier against foolishness. Even the old man needs wisdom. We may be old and foolish.

The ultimate lesson is that wisdom does not come naturally with the addition of years or even by might (16:32). The benefit of wisdom does not depend on our effort or on our status. It is a sovereign act of "chance." Strangely, the concept of chance is suggested here. The wise man refers to the custom of casting lots (16:33). The ancient Israelites, like their neighbors, played games of chance. They probably used marked pebbles in order to determine the right choice to make. In biblical civilization, however, casting lots was often used as a way to inquire of God's will about a particular dilemma, such as the choice of a king (1 Sam. 10:19ff.), the detection of a culprit (Josh. 7:10–18; Jon. 1:7), or the distribution of land (Isa. 34:17; Ezek. 45:1; 47:22). The point of our proverb is that, whatever our choices, the outcome belongs completely to God. Solomon refers to the same "chance" in his other book, when he says, "The race is not to the swift, nor the battle to the strong, nor bread to the wise, nor riches to men of understanding, nor favor to men of skill; but time and chance happen to them all" (Eccles. 9:11).

This lesson may sound odd in the context of the Holy Scriptures. Yet this is a powerful statement about God's sovereignty. From the point of view of Proverbs and Ecclesiastes, wisdom—like any form of success—is not the product of our own human effort but is essentially a sovereign act of grace on God's part.

CHAPTER 7

The Price for Peace

The wise man continues, now talking about the strange fact that often those who care the most about religion are often in conflict with people. We may have a rich religious life, and know a lot of theology, and even give a lot of money to the church, and yet we always cause conflict with others. The wise man of Proverbs says, better than "feasting" and having "sacrificial meals" (17:1)[1] filled with strife is the hunger of the simple church member who lives in peace with his neighbor (17:1).

After having emphasized the importance of the sovereignty of God and having urged his son to make God a priority, Solomon then warns him against the dangers of war. For the crusades and the jihad often go hand in hand with zeal for God. After a lesson about God, we then need to be trained in conflict management. This construction of peace is not easy, for peace is not compromise, but as the Hebrew word for "peace" (*shalom*) implies, it demands integrity instead. We cannot build peace on the surface. We first need to work in our heart to catch the problem at its root. Then we need to move outside of ourselves and live with the other people. To be holy alone does not count. We have to be holy in the company of others.

---

1. The Hebrew word means literally "sacrificial meal."

The wise man of Proverbs does not promote the monastic life. For him, holiness excludes separateness. We will then have to listen to each other. The silence of the saint is not the silence of the desert where there is no human being, but it is the silence within the community, where the other is present and speaks loudly. It is the silence that carries the risk to convey the words that will shake us. Peace will be achieved at this price.

The root of the problem

The first requirement for the construction of genuine peace concerns our intimate motivations: who we really are. It is not enough to be brothers and sisters. What is important is the heart. For instance, a wise slave could be more worthy to inherit than a son who "causes shame" (17:2). The real value of a man should not be measured by the quality of his watch or the size of his house or by the sign of nobility attached to his name or by the great schools he has attended, but by his heart. This is the scale of values by which Samuel is supposed to choose the right king for Israel: "The LORD does not see as man sees; for man looks at the outward appearance, but the LORD looks at the heart" (1 Sam. 16:7). This is the point of Proverbs: "The LORD tests the hearts" (17:3b). The process suggested by the Hebrew verb *bkhn,* for "test," implies a thorough searching (Ps. 139:23), such as the one implemented in the metallurgical industry (17:3a). There is no room here for lies and hypocrisy.

On the opposite side are those who value only what they see, the immediate appearance and the present enjoyment. They despise the poor (17:5a) and mock the calamity that strikes them (17:5b) because they believe that their poverty is evidence of their own superiority over them. Their indifference and their insensitivity angers God, who associates Himself with the poor (17:5a). They elaborate on the sin of the poor (17:9a), for it justifies their contempt and establishes their own self-righteousness. This attitude disrupts social harmony (17:9b; cf. 17:11) too. We cannot go back anymore.

This fool is not aware of the damage of his slander and the danger it represents. The wise man compares him to "a bear robbed of her cubs" (17:12). We cannot reason with a bear that has lost all her lucidity and her discernment; she returns evil for good (17:13) and has now become dangerous. The wise man concludes that the only solution to that problem is prevention: "Stop contention before a quarrel starts" (17:14).

Note that the advice is not to stop the contention at the beginning but before it even starts. The wise man does not resort to the contingency of politics; he refers, instead, to a spiritual principle. The wise man had mentioned "love" as the primary solution (17:9). The covering of transgression is not a cover-up because we fear that disclosure will compromise the future administrative position of that person. The Hebrew expression belongs to the language of forgiveness (Ps. 32:1). The covering is an act of forgiveness; it implies the recognition of the sin and the unequivocal rebuke (17:10). Here love goes along with justice.

Now, with the question of justice, we have to make sure that one does not justify the wicked and condemn the innocent (17:15, 26). The essence of this principle is to avoid focusing on wickedness: "He who loves transgression loves strife" (17:19). Some people are keen on noticing the transgression of others. They do not commit the transgression, but they like watching for it in others. The reason for this paradoxical attitude is within themselves: they have a distorted mind, a "crooked heart" (17:20, NLT). The only way to produce a good and healthy society is to work on our heart. If there is joy in our heart we will bring health and *shalom* to our body and our society (17:22a). If there is bitterness in our heart we will bring sickness to our flesh and conflict to the world (17:22b).

The solution to our problem is very close: "Wisdom is in the sight of him who has understanding" (17:24a). And even with wisdom, the temptation is to think that magic words will solve the problem. The wise man warns us against this fallacy. The best and only way to prevent strife and promote peace is very simple and brutal: "Shut up!" The wise man explains that the expression of wisdom is not the quality of our words but *the sparing* of our words (17:27a). The wise man urges us to think before speaking and to control our mind (17:27b). Even if we are naturally foolish, recommends the wise one, silence is the right option because, in that case, it will change the fool into a wise person (17:28). Even if we do not know what to say, and especially if we know what to say, silence remains the best formula.

Lonely is not holy

The ideal of the wise of Proverbs is not the seclusion of the monastery and the solitude of the desert. To be holy, we have to live with the others. I learned this lesson early in my life. One day, I was sitting, nice and quiet, in my father's little bookbinding shop. My father was puzzled by my perfect behavior. He asked me the question: "How come you are a saint here, and when you are at home you become a demon?"

The answer came spontaneously to my lips: "At home I am with my brothers and sisters" (we were two brothers and two sisters).

It was the perfect opportunity for my father to teach me a lesson about the meaning of holiness. The saint is not the one who flees to a mountain but the one who lives well with others. The wise man of Proverbs unveils once again the secret motivation of the heart: "A man who isolates himself seeks his own desire" (18:1a). The achievement of holiness is not the real reason he sought loneliness. The real reason is selfishness. No one will disrupt him in his desires; no one will contradict him; no one will bother him.

The wise man suggests that the wisdom he gets in those conditions is suspect (18:1b). The person who separates himself from others thinks of himself as superior over others. He is not interested "in understanding" (18:2). On the contrary, "he rages" against other opinions, especially wise and right opinions, because they threaten him. He is interested only in his own point of view (18:2b). Contempt is second nature to him (18:3a). An earlier proverb had anticipated the danger represented by the lonely man: "He who builds a high gate invites destruction" (17:19b, NIV). The meaning of this proverb has diverse applications, including the allusion to the concrete threat of a possible invasion. It gives ideas to the bandit who suspects a great treasure. The bandit will, then, break into the house to find it. In our context of Proverbs the lesson warns us against the lonely man. This man will bring destruction. The thinking of that man is compared to "deep waters" (18:4a). It seems "deep" because it does not move. No pebble has disturbed its surface. This water is unhealthy and should not be drunk. On the other hand, wisdom is compared to "a flowing brook" (18:4). It does not stand still. It is always fresh, always renewed from the rain above or the moving water.

It is important, therefore, to exert good judgment and apply discernment. The folly of the wicked should be denounced as such and not be deemed as wisdom (18:5a). Conversely, the point of view of wisdom should be acknowledged as wise and should be promoted (18:5b). In matters of wisdom, diplomacy is not always appropriate. Yet the wise does not confront the fool; he does not engage in a debate with him to show him and the world that he is wrong. Again, silence is his tool. For the fool who has not tested the truth of his words will reveal himself as a fool through his own words (18:6–8). He will reveal his ignorance.

A number of precious guidelines are then set down to help the seeker of wisdom as opposed to the actions of the fool. First, consider the wisdom of others; hear "a matter" before you speak and offer your point of view (18:13). The other person may be right and you may be wrong. In that case, suggests the wise man, instead of lecturing, listen and learn (18:15). You will benefit from that act of listening (18:16). The wise man suggests going even further in that experience. Do not just content yourself with one opinion. Ask for a second opinion: "The first one to plead his cause seems right, until his neighbor comes and examines him" (18:17). The apostle Paul resonates with this wisdom: "Test all things; hold fast what is good" (1 Thess. 5:21).

Yet this confrontation can be difficult and risky. The wise man warns of one potential problem. We may lose a friend in that process (18:19). Thus he suggests that you two agree on one common criterion for truth. For that purpose, he refers to casting lots (18:18). The fundamental idea is that only God has the absolute answer to that question. For the book of Proverbs, there is an absolute truth that transcends all the other opinions and that should be chosen by all. This specific type of consultation, however, was possible only in biblical times. God, in His generosity, consented to speak directly through this process. The people had nothing else.

Today, this method would not be appropriate, not only because if does not fit our civilization but also because God has provided us with other systems that did not exist then, namely the voice of Scripture and the experience of history.

As we have seen, holiness implies the presence of others who sometimes challenge us to think and act differently. A friend is necessary in the quest for wisdom and in the construction of a peaceful society, because his company will refine our character and force us to the exercise of respect and politeness (18:24a). In fact, the friend is sometimes more faithful than a brother or sister (18:24b) because he is with us and for us freely, not because of his family obligations.

The value of the poor

The shift to the topic of the poor at this juncture (19:1) may surprise us but is not irrelevant. We will naturally listen to the close friend or to the beloved wife. But we tend to push away (19:4, 7b) or even hate the poor (19:7a). We think that the poor has nothing to contribute to our happiness and our wisdom.

We are making a big mistake in this attitude. First, the wise man warns us against the deception of appearances. The observation of a rich fool and a poor wise man is upsetting and confusing; for this should be the other way around: "Luxury is not fitting for a fool" (19:10). But the condition of poverty has nothing to do with the lack of wisdom, and the status of riches has nothing to do with the possession of wisdom. The poor may be poor because he refuses to cheat, because he "walks in his integrity" (19:1a), unlike this other person who may be successful and rich but "is perverse in his lips" and a fool (19:1b).

Paradoxically, this deceptive association contains an important lesson about the authenticity of wisdom. That wisdom is connected with poverty is actually the sign of true wisdom. For it is free from any false pretentions. If we go to a wise poor one to learn about wisdom, it is wisdom we are interested in and nothing else, since the wise poor man has nothing else to offer but his wisdom. If wisdom is associated with money, we will seek for wisdom not because we value wisdom but because we value money. We will not get wisdom under those conditions. We will get money and forget about wisdom.

This is why we are encouraged to have this grace, this act of free and disinterested attention to the poor: lend to the poor (19:17). Learn to think that you will have something in return from the poor, although it seems that nothing could come from him. This act of faith toward this other human is assured with a promise from the Lord Himself. If we give to the poor, knowing very well that we will not get reimbursed, it is God Himself who will return the debt. Besides being an economic encouragement to relieve the poor in our society, this proverb implies an attitude that concerns the intrinsic value of wisdom. The only vital thing that counts is wisdom. This is repeated over and over again in our passage: "He who gets wisdom loves his own soul" (19:8; cf. 19:2, 16, 27).

At the same time, the case of lending to the poor illustrates another important principle in the pedagogy of wisdom. Although we seem to invest at a loss, we will get the money back much later. The reward of wisdom is never immediate: "Listen to counsel and receive instruction, that you may be wise in your latter days" (19:20). Education is the key for the future: "Discipline your children, for in that there is hope" (19:18, NIV). Likewise, what makes the value of a wife over inheritance is precisely the potential future that she represents. There is more of a future with a good wife than with a lot of money (19:14). Conversely, the future is the test that shows the wrong behavior.

The wise man provides a list of typical examples to support his case. The lazy person who lives only in the present will have no future. He sleeps or buries his hand in a bowl and will therefore die by starvation (19:15, 24). The scoffer who does not respect his father and his mother (19:26), refuses to listen to their instruction (19:27), and does not care about truth (19:28) will have for the future only judgments and beatings (19:25, 29). The solution, then, is to reprove that scoffer and teach him to be prudent and foresee the potential risk that lies in the future (19:25). The training of wisdom is to learn to think about the future. Survival depends on wisdom: "He who has it will abide in satisfaction" (19:23).

CHAPTER 8

Looking for Man

There is a story about the Greek philosopher Diogenes, who strolled about in full daylight with a lamp. When he was asked what he was doing, he answered: "I am just looking for a man." What Diogenes meant in this strange mime is not clear. For sure, Diogenes was desperate; he could not find what he was looking for. Jesus seemed to share the same pessimism when He asked the rhetorical question: "When the Son of Man comes, will He really find faith on the earth?" (Luke 18:8). In all these vain queries, which convey the same hopeless question, one expects the same painful answer: there is no such a man. In that sense we are all equal. So, whatever you think about yourself, even if you are the best among your peers, even if you are a holy man devoted to the highest sacrifices, your worth as a man will be defined by what is left of you when you are no longer around. Indeed, your worth can be measured by what you have sowed.

You are like them

Equality between human beings is one of the most difficult concepts to grasp. If we look at each other, we see that we are not equal. He is stronger and bigger than I am. She is more intelligent than he is. They are richer than we are. We are more spiritual than you are. And

79

yet this principle is vital for the survival of our society. Differences are good: "The hearing ear and the seeing eye, the LORD has made both of them" (20:12). The same lesson will be repeated later and applied to age differences: "The glory of young men is their strength, and the splendor of old men is their gray head" (20:29); and to social categories: "The rich and the poor have this in common, the LORD is the maker of them all" (22:2).

The reference to the Creator is not just a pious excuse to inspire our respect of the other person; it is essentially a statement about the unique value of the other person, because their difference has been created by God. The equality that is affirmed here is not just an administrative decree that we must apply as civilized people because it is politically correct. Instead, for Proverbs, these differences are in vital need of each other, just as the eye and the ear, the young and the old, the rich and the poor; and (we could add in the same spirit) the farmer and the student, the woman and the man, the African and the European, the Gentile and the Jew. What makes our equality *is* our difference.

You are not what you think

The mocker stands again on the scene. The same mocker who mistreated his father and mother (19:26), despised their instructions (19:27), and was not interested in the truth (19:28) is now drinking and bragging about himself. Wine is now adding to his euphoria. A rabbinic story describes the stages of degradation caused by drinking. In the beginning you feel like a powerful lion; no one can stand before you. You are the greatest. Then you become like a pig, eating just anything and rolling in the filth. And finally you are like a monkey, dancing around and completely unaware of what you are doing (*Tanhuma, Noah* 14).

The drinking mocker is now at the stage of the lion (20:2). He has a very high idea of himself and therefore provokes anyone who thinks differently than he does (20:2–3). The point of Proverbs is not so much to warn us against the trap of wine drinking and its deception, although it conveys that message also. The wise intends here to denounce those who brag and entertain the illusion of their own superiority. For the wise man, they are like this drunkard.

The first criticism is that they are delusional and have totally lost their sense of reality. According to the wise man, this disease concerns "most men" (20:6). They all "proclaim" that they are good people. The Hebrew verb *qr'* for "proclaim" means also "read loud" (Deut. 7:19), "cry with a loud voice" (Ezek. 8:18). They have become masters in marketing. They promote themselves loudly at home, in the office, and in the marketplace. It looks like a political campaign.

According to the wise man, though, they are lying about themselves, for "who can find a faithful man?" (20:6), implying that there is no such man. The same thought rebounds when the man boasts that his heart is clean and that he did not sin (20:9). Not only does he think of himself as the best, he is also unaware of his mistakes. This is self-delusion. The book of Ecclesiastes warns: "There is not a just man on earth who does good and does not sin" (Eccles. 7:20). Likewise, Jesus specifies that "no one is good but One, that is, God" (Matt. 19:17). The man thinks that all his ways are right; he is perfect in all he does and plans to do. The wise warns us, then, against the one who boasts and claims that he has all the answers and understands all the secrets (20:19), when in fact he does not even know who he is (20:24).

We should beware of these people who have their way with words. Their speech is deceiving. The wise man applies his counsel to the concrete situation of life, when we are in great need of sound counsel (20:18), when we make plans or when we want to engage in a war. We should not trust the buyer who bargains and pretends that the merchandise is not good, and buys it at a good price and then boasts about the good deal (20:14). The same holds with flattery (20:19). The one who likes to boast likes to be flattered and uses the art of flattery to get what he wants.

But what matters are not words but deeds. While the fool, like the sluggard, speaks a lot and does nothing (20:4), the righteous does not say a word; instead, he just "walks in his integrity" (20:7a). This test works already at a very early stage of life: "Even a child is known by his deeds" (20:11). For the abundance and the rhetoric of words often hide the emptiness of the heart and cover the lack of actions. This criticism is particularly pertinent in our culture of mass media, where the sensational and the loud often compensate for the insignificance of our work. Ironically, the shaping of these talkative and boasting reports sometimes takes more time and more energy (if not more money) than does the actual work itself.

There can be great iniquity behind such deceitful boasting. We raise funds and receive compliments for something we have not done and we are not doing. The wise man concludes his evaluation with the prospect of judgment. Even if our beautiful words have deceived our audience, even if we have deceived ourselves, "the LORD weighs the hearts" (21:2); for it is only the action that counts. Jesus resonates with this warning when He alerts some of the Pharisees of His time who liked to boast about their piety but did nothing: "Not everyone who says to Me, 'Lord, Lord,' shall enter the kingdom of heaven, but he who does the will of My Father in heaven" (Matt. 7:21).

You are not what you pray

Some people may push their art of deception even further. They use religion to hide their wickedness or lack of action. They are zealous in their sacrifices and yet they do not "do righteousness and justice" (21:3). This scandalous incoherence shocked the prophet Micah, who confronted his contemporaries by exposing what was going on. Many were eager to go to the sacred altar and offer the best sacrifices, yet Micah dismisses their offerings. The only thing God wants from you, he said, is "to do justly, to love mercy" (Mic. 6:8). James will repeat the same lesson: "Pure and undefiled religion before God and the father is this: to visit orphans and widows in their trouble" (James 1:27).

The wise man of Proverbs defines religion in the same terms; he lists a long series of actions and attitudes that concern the way we relate to others. Significantly, he begins his curriculum with the problem of our ego. Pride is the first issue to address (21:4). He calls it "sin" when we look down on people and think of ourselves as more important; it's what the wise man calls (with a bit of irony) "the lamp of the wicked" (21:4, NASB). Proverbs preaches to those who flock to churches, synagogues, and mosques. The author observes that these religious people get rich in lying to their customers (21:6); are violent (21:7), perverse (21:8), and in conflict with their spouse (21:9) and their neighbor (21:10); ignore the shout of the poor (21:13); accept bribes (21:14); love pleasures (21:17); and covet all day long (21:26). For him, the religion of these people is "an abomination" (21:27), a word that implies God's strong reprobation and repulsion (15:8). A religion that comes with the rejection of others is bound to be rejected by the great Other. It is preferable in this case not to be religious at all.

The wise man then concludes his point with the consideration that the situation is even worse than first thought: they are not just being inconsistent; they use religion to promote their wickedness (21:27). For them, religion is a means to fulfill their own wicked plans. We may think of the business-oriented minister who exploits the religious feelings of his parishioners to build a personal fortune or to abuse children and women. But we may also think of those individuals who use religion to promote their social status or to obtain a job. More dramatically, this criticism concerns those religious people who commit crimes for religious reasons: the church treasurer who falsifies the accounts in order to enrich the church; the evangelist who lies in his testimony in order to promote the diffusion of the Gospel; the anti-Semitic crusader or the jihadist or the religious settler who hates and kills in the name of God. For the wise man, such an attitude is more than an abomination (21:27).

You are what you sow

It is neither the past nor the present that really defines us, or rather tests who we are; it is the future. Proverbs has already touched on this idea in connection to the idea of survival. What makes the crown of old men who will die very soon is not their past or present actions that they could boast about; it is what will survive them in the future: "Children's children are the crown of old men" (17:6). The value of the righteous man is measured only in the future: "His children are blessed after him" (20:7).

The book of Revelation notes this paradox about the saints who "die in the Lord": "their deeds will follow them" (Rev. 14:13, NIV). This principle, which was hinted at before, is now developed in various respects. The person who gives a false testimony will perish, but the effect of that word will have no end (21:28). A "good name" is preferable over "great riches" (22:1). In his other book, Solomon refers to the same priority: "A good name is better than precious ointment" (Eccles. 7:1). The point is that the "name" that evokes the reputation of the person is the only element that survives the person after his/her death. The ancient Egyptians, who were very concerned about their afterlife, built great monuments where their names were etched in stone. One of the Hebrew words for monument, *yad washem* (literally, "a place and a name"), testifies to the same preoccupation (Isa. 56:5).

This principle is the basis for education: "Train up a child in the way he should go, and when he is old he will not depart from it" (22:6). What we are depends on what we have received when young. The Hebrew word *khnk* for "train," which refers to the work of education, is also the technical word for "dedication" (1 Kings 8:63), which contains the idea of early beginnings. When we educate a child, we give them, from the very beginning, a special orientation that will shape their identity. Natural foolishness can be corrected only in childhood; after that it is too late (22:15). Education implies faith and hope, that is, the capacity to see the potential of the child, to believe in him, and then to build accordingly.

The same way of thinking is recognized in the act of charity. The person who gives to the poor does so with the future in mind, because he has that "bountiful eye" that allows him to see the potential relief of the needy (22:9). Education, like charity, "hopes all things" (1 Cor. 13:7) and as such is a ministry of love. The counterpart of this attitude is found in the person who oppresses the poor and favors the rich (22:16). It is because this man does not see the future with the poor, while he sees the future with the rich, that he impoverishes the poor and enriches the rich. The man behaves that way because he is unable to see the future; he identifies the future with the present. Paradoxically, this behavior, which relies only on the present, will have no future: the person who does that with the purpose of getting rich will end up poor (22:16b).

The underlying principle is that we reap what we sow (22:8), in the good as well as in the bad. The challenge is that no one knows what we will reap. We know only the seed that we sow; and this seed has no identity per se. When we see a seed, we do not know *a priori* if it is the seed of a rose or the seed of grass. Only the plant that has grown and blossomed has an identity. The problem is that we have to wait until we know.

Unfortunately, our impatience and our inability to wait is the main reason why we sin. The person who cannot wait through many years of hard work to be rich will abuse the poor and care only for the rich (22:16); he may also lie and deceive his customers (21:5). The student who cannot wait through several years of painful learning will cheat and falsify a diploma. Proverbs warns us against the temptation of the quick fix. Haste leads to poverty (21:5). We want to expedite an inheritance in order to ensure our immediate substantial benefit (20:21); we do not care about the siblings who will lose their fair share. The result will be a long and drawn-out legal battle that we will lose and, hence, be poorer than before.

We rush into an act of revenge because we need to enjoy right away the punishment of our enemy. Proverbs appeals here to our faith and our religious hope: "Wait for the LORD" (20:22). The desire for an immediate response to the person who harmed us is natural and deeply felt. The *lex talionis*, "eye for eye and tooth for tooth" (Exod. 21:24), which was designed to be a mere pedagogical formula for learning to love our neighbor as ourselves, has often been used to legitimize our violence. Ironically, Jesus restored its original intention in turning what was understood as a call for revenge into an act of love: "Whoever slaps you on your right cheek, turn the other to him also. If anyone wants to sue you and take away your tunic, let him have your cloak also. And whoever compels you to go one mile, go with him two. . . . You shall . . . love your enemies, bless those who curse you" (Matt. 5:38–44). This lesson is one of the most difficult to accept and to apply. That the proverb promises salvation if we "wait for the Lord" is particularly meaningful; for our revenge will not bring salvation but only more trouble. Our problem is that we cannot wait; we want our salvation right away, and therefore we miss it. The baker who wants to bake a cake and cannot wait for the leaven to rise will get only a flatbread. Our civilization of speed-reading and fast food badly needs to recover this important virtue.

CHAPTER 9

The House on the Rock

The parable of Jesus could be heard through the sayings of the wise: "Whoever hears these sayings of Mine, and does them, I will liken him to a wise man who built his house on the rock" (Matt. 7:24). Likewise, the wise man of Proverbs urges us to trust the Lord and to build our house on the rock. In this new section of the book, "the words of the wise" develop in two parts. The first part (22:17–24:22), after some preliminaries regarding the need for wisdom in our heart (22:17–21), lists a series of "thirty sayings" (22:20, NLT, NIV)[1] consisting of specific instructions concerning our concrete behavior in life: our work ethics, our eating and drinking, our family, our neighbor, and our government. What is interesting is that Solomon has, as we said at the beginning, deliberately drawn some of the material of his sayings from an Egyptian source, "The Instruction of Amenemope." The reason for this borrowing is not that the biblical author has lost his inspiration. The reason is that the biblical author found the truth and the value of

---

1. The thirty sayings are grouped according to the following distribution: (1) 22:21–23; (2) 22:24–25; (3) 22:26–27; (4) 22:28; (5) 22:29; (6) 23:1–3; (7) 23:4–5; (8) 23:6–8; (9) 23:9; (10) 23:10–11; (11) 23:12; (12) 23:13–14; (13) 23:15–16; (14) 23:17–18; (15) 23:19–21; (16) 23:22–25; (17) 23:26–28; (18) 23:29–35; (19) 24:1–2; (20) 24:3–4; (21) 24:5–6; (22) 24:7; (23) 24:8–9; (24) 24:10; (25) 24:11–12; (26) 24:13–14; (27) 24:15–16; (28) 24:17–18; (29) 24:19–20; (30) 24:21–22; cf. Duane Garret, *Proverbs, Ecclesiastes, Songs of Songs*, vol. 14, New American Commentary (Nashville: B & H Publishing Group, 1993), 193–200.

this "secular" ethics truth that God must have revealed to its author. Even the pagan and the atheist owe their wisdom to God.

The wise one of Proverbs states explicitly the purpose of his sayings: "so that your trust may be in the LORD" (22:19). The second part (24:23–34) seems to be different from the first. The style is different: there is no reference to the trust in the Lord, and yet the wise man pursues the same wisdom. We should not seek to judge based on own subjective "partiality" (24:23–25, 28–29) or build our house on the surface of our "field" (24:27, 30–34). We should instead judge our case on the basis of solid evidence or build our house upon a thorough preparation of its foundation.

Don't do it!

The religion that is affirmed here is not made of religious beliefs or of theological statements; it is made of tangible "don't do it" statements that concern our daily life. The religious truth promoted here should be tested in the flesh of our existence.

The Depth of Wisdom. The words of the wise man should be well received in our heart and overflow to our lips (22:17–19) in such a way that the certainty of their truth may be acknowledged by those who hear it (22:21–22). The efficiency of our verbal testimony depends, then, essentially on how the truth has been received in our heart. To make his point clear, the wise man compares wisdom to honey that is eaten and enjoyed: "Eat honey because it is good, . . . sweet to your taste; so shall the knowledge of wisdom be to your soul" (24:13). Before being on the lips, wisdom has to be well assimilated. What counts first is that the words "upon our lips" be deeply rooted in our understanding.

The wise teacher begins with the premise: "Apply your heart to my knowledge" (22:17). What counts more than anything is wisdom in our heart. This basic requirement is repeated throughout this discourse: "Apply your heart to instruction" (23:12); "Do not let your heart envy sinners" (23:17), to which is attached the promise of eternal life (23:18);

"Buy the truth, . . . also wisdom and instruction and understanding" (23:23). The reason for this emphasis is explicitly stated in metaphoric language in sayings twenty (24:3–4) and twenty-one (24:5–6), where the process of adoption of wisdom is compared to the building of a house: "Through wisdom a house is built" (24:3). Wisdom is what guarantees the solidity of the house, just as the house built on the rock is solid (Matt. 7:24). So pursue wisdom if you want to guarantee success in your enterprise, even the most risky ones, such as war.

Base your endeavors not on strength but on wisdom (24:5)—a well-tested wisdom through the consultation of many counselors (24:6). As the ancient rabbis of the Talmud used to say: "Rivalry between sages increases wisdom" (*Baba Batra* 21a). This deep commitment to wisdom is very demanding. The wise man is aware of the difficulty of that requirement, and his teaching is often punctuated with doubts that his pupil will ever adopt it. The wise man, like other teachers, is discouraged to see that the high value of his teaching is often despised or doesn't fit with what people want. It's like "a ring of gold in swine's snout" (11:22), or "pearls before swine" (Matt. 7:6). The wise one sighs, then, and feels hopeless before this challenge: "Wisdom is too lofty for a fool" (24:7). But he does not lower his standards and does not compromise with the push of mediocrity. The wise man still insists that unless wisdom reaches our heart and affects all the aspects of our life, it is false wisdom.

Our Work Ethic. Laziness is one of the sins that the wise man of Proverbs had already warned us against (6:6–11; 10:4; 15:19; 19:15, etc.). Just a few verses before, we heard his mocking of the lazy person who fears work as one would fear the threatening lion (22:13). Work is therefore praised as an important value to pursue: "Do you see a man who excels in his work? He will stand before kings" (22:29). It is not enough to work; we must "excel" in our work. Yet, work should be monitored. Otherwise it could harm others and even us. We should not work against people, and especially at the expense of the unemployed, who are poor and vulnerable (22:22) and ready to accept all our conditions because they have no other choice.

In our modern societies this abuse has been and is still practiced. We think of the illegal or legal alien who is abused in some of the wealthiest companies. Or think of child labor, where kids are employed with very low wages that help make the rich richer. We may also think of the shrewd strategies of the multinationals, which hire foreign workers at a low rate and in inhuman conditions. On a larger scale, we may also include the exploitation of colonization and of slavery, whereby the richer countries took advantage of the poor and underdeveloped countries to enrich themselves. The wise man also denounces any attempt on the part of the avid rich to "remove the ancient landmark" (23:10; cf. 22:28) or take advantage of a property that would belong to the fatherless.

He warns us, too, against the harm that work may cause to ourselves. However valuable our work and our commitment to high quality may be, we should not work at the expense of our health or of our family life: "Do not overwork" (23:4). The intention of this exaggeration has nothing to do with the need for work or the demands of excellence; it is simply "to be rich" (23:4). The wise argues that wealth is not worth that sacrifice; and it will "fly away" (23:5). The enjoyment of the riches we acquire will not last, and our riches will disappear anyway (cf. Eccles. 6:2). The wise man urges this workaholic to "cease" (23:4), because he has reached a dangerous point. The same verb is used to describe the builders of the tower of Babel when they "ceased building the city" (Gen. 11:8).

Our Eating and Drinking. The same counsel for moderation is applied to the way we eat and drink. To the person who likes to eat much, the wise one advises: "Put a knife to your throat" (23:2). This call for self-control refers to the situation of the guests, for it is not polite to eat too much when we are invited. We would even lose the respect of our host, and his delicious food could then be "deceptive" (23:3) and become the occasion for our fall. Yet, this counsel goes beyond the particular situation of a guest and concerns more generally the glutton.

The "knife on the throat" image is a dramatic measure, which ironically fits this case. The image is particularly suggestive. The knife on the throat of the eater not only keeps the food from going farther down the throat, but it also threatens his life. The glutton is in danger of death. Eating too much could indeed cost the glutton his life. Note, however, that the wise does not advocate an ascetic rule of life; he even encourages eating honey "because it is good" (24:13). The problem he fights is intemperance.

Drinking wine takes a special place in the book of Proverbs, as exemplified here. Although he associates the glutton and the drunkard in the same judgment (they both lead to poverty [23:21]), the wise devotes a whole satiric poem to the wine drinker (23:29–35). This suggests a different danger that does not concern the glutton. While the glutton is warned at the stage of his gluttony, when he eats too much, the wine drinker is warned at a very early stage, when he just looks "on the wine when it is red," and when the cup is not yet drunk (23:31). To discourage us from wine drinking, we are told of a series of consequences: "woe," "sorrow," "contentions," "complaints," and "wounds without cause" (23:29). The wise even predicts the last stage of wine drinking ("At the last it bites like a serpent" [23:32]) and anticipates the sorrow of the alcoholic (24:35). While the wise man of Proverbs recommends moderation and self-control in regard to food, he opts for total abstinence in regard to wine. The reason for this radical option is the potential menace of alcoholism. Alcoholism is the reason for abstention.

Our Family. The happiness of families depends on both the relationship between husband and wife and the relationship between parents and children. It is interesting that the two relationships are set in connection to each other. The call to refrain from engaging in adulterous relations follows immediately the call to honor one's father and mother (23:22) and rejoice in them (23:24–25). This is all rooted in the quality of his relationship with his father and in the father's behavior as a role model: "My son, give me your heart, and let your eyes observe my ways" (23:26).

Our Neighbor. We are responsible for our neighbors. Jesus' parable of the good Samaritan (Luke 10:33–37) not only teaches us who is our neighbor (Luke 10:36–37) but also obliges us to takes action to save our neighbor when he is in peril. The story of the rescue of three thousand Jews, most of them children, at Le Chambon-sur-Lignon, a Protestant village of the Cévennes region in France during the Holocaust, illustrates the point of Proverbs. The Jews were staying in the houses of the inhabitants and on their isolated farms. When the Germans came, the Jews fled into the woods. In 1988 Le Chambon-sur-Lignon received the official name of "Righteous Among the Nations" for this act of heroism, which involved all the inhabitants of the village and their pastor.

Unfortunately, this kind of courage was rare, and many people preferred to keep quiet before the massacres. Many justified their silence and their passivity on the pretext that they did not know. The author of Proverbs has this kind of people in mind when he says: "If you say, 'Surely we did not know this,' does not He who weighs the hearts consider it?" (24:12). Along with this inspired warning, a famous statement and provocative poem attributed to Pastor Martin Niemöller (1892–1984) warns against the cowardice that characterized the response of many German intellectuals to the rise of Nazism, simply because they did not feel concerned about it:

> First they came for the Socialists, and I did not speak out—
> Because I was not a Socialist.
> Then they came for the Trade Unionists, and I did not speak out—
> Because I was not a Trade Unionist.
> Then they came for the Jews, and I did not speak out—
> Because I was not a Jew.

Just like the Samaritan of the parable and the inhabitants of Le Chambon-sur-Lignon, we are responsible for our neighbor, and we should feel concerned about their misery. Paradoxically, between the wise prudence of the coward, who says that he does not know, and the risky actions of the righteous, the book of Proverbs opts for the latter.

Pessimistically, the wise one predicts that the attitude of the righteous does not pay: "The righteous fall seven times" (24:16a, NIV). On the other hand, the attitude of the wicked seems to pay: "The wicked shall fall" (24:16b). While the righteous falls seven times, the wicked falls only once. The fundamental difference, however, is that the righteous will rise again seven times, while the wicked falls only once because he does not rise again. Courage is therefore a part of the program of wisdom: "If you faint in the day of adversity, your strength is small" (24:10). This proverb is not just observing the unavoidable outcome of a weak character; it is an encouragement not to "faint" in the day of struggles and fears; otherwise we will lose our strength.

It is the practice of resistance and strength that increases our strength. The Hebrew verse could also be translated: "If you are weak in the day of trouble, you will get weak." There is a play on words here between the word *trouble* (*tsarah*) and the following word *weak* (*tsar*), suggesting that the weak is dependent in the event of trouble. The lesson of wisdom hidden in this play on words is that we should not let the events determine our position.

The extreme case of the fall of our enemy could serve as an illustration for this principle: "Do not rejoice when your enemy falls" (24:17). Although this reflex would just be natural, the wise man denounces it as a behavior that would "displease" the Lord (24:18). We are warned that if we enjoy the misfortune of our enemy, it is as if we participate in that troubling event, and God will therefore "turn away His wrath from him" (24:18; cf. 15:1).

Our Government. The king represents the highest authority on earth; we should respect this authority as we do the Lord Himself (cf. Matt. 22:21). The intention of this association between the king and the Lord is not just to justify our civil duties; it is also a veiled warning directed at the son, the future king, namely that the king owes his authority to God and is therefore subject to His Law (Deut. 17:14–20; cf. Eccles. 5:8–9).

Proverbs

Prepare the field

This brief appendix (24:23–34), which is also attributed to the wise man (24:23), focuses on a particular aspect of his teaching, namely the need to go in depth in our judgment and in our work. The wise man warns against, on the one hand, the temptation of "partiality in judgment" (24:23–26) and in false witnessing (24:28–29), and on the other, the temptation of superficiality in our work (24:27, 30–34). The two temptations are presented in a chiastic fashion:

- Partiality in judgment (24:23–26)
- Superficiality in building (24:27)
- Partiality in being a witness (24:28–29)
- Superficiality in culture (24:30–34)

Partiality. The primary application of this counsel is the legal court and concerns the judge (24:23–26) or the witness (24:28–29), who may be tempted to support or reject a case not on the basis of truth but on the basis of their relationship or past experience with the person. Beyond this concrete legal context, however, the principle here may also apply to our daily life, on the way we judge and treat our neighbor.

The doctrine of the two ways underlies this ethic. It is important that good and evil are clearly recognized as such. It is of course in the interest of the righteous to acknowledge his innocence, for this will strengthen and encourage his commitment to righteousness. But it is also in the interest of the wicked, for it will take him to repentance. It is also in the interest of the judge and the witness to utter the right judgment or the right testimony, for this "right answer kisses the lips" (24:26) and thus silences all the parties involved (see Gen. 41:40).

Besides, to call the righteous wicked and the wicked righteous (24:24–25) stands against the very nature of wisdom, which consists precisely in discerning between good and evil (1 Kings 3:9). The Deuteronomic view of blessings and curses, associated respectively with obedience or disobedience to the Law of God, reinforces this dichotomy between the two orders (Deut. 27:11–28:68) and turns this human judgment into the divine judgment (Eccles. 12:14). The lesson of the recommendation is the assurance of the presence of God on our side as we apply this wisdom of discernment and the redeeming promise of God's judgment.

Superficiality. The wise one warns us against the temptation of easy or busy work that in reality leads nowhere. When we build a house, we must first work on the foundations, the parts that no one will see and admire. Our eagerness to be quickly recognized and praised and our impatience to enjoy as soon as possible the result of our work may incite us to focus only on the visible parts. Sooner or later the bad quality of our work will be revealed. Very soon the thorns of the field will swallow any vineyard that has not been thoroughly and truly taken care of (24:30–31), and our poverty will catch us like a thief (24:34). The same fate awaits the house easily built on soft sand: "The rain descended, the floods came, and the winds blew and beat on that house; and it fell. And great was its fall" (Matt. 7:27).

CHAPTER 10

Coping With the Other Person

"The more I see of people, the more I like my dog." This quote, attributed to Mark Twain, has been said with some variations by many people—from Roman writer Seneca some two thousand years ago to Charles de Gaulle in the twentieth century. This cynical observation expresses how difficult it is to deal with our fellow men and women and how disappointing they are sometimes. Yet, we have to cope with them, just as they have to cope with us. This new section of proverbs (25–29), which originated also with Solomon and was compiled by King Hezekiah and his scribes (25:1), devotes it first part (25–27) to the unavoidable necessity of learning how to deal with others. We need to cope with all the people who surround us, even those who make our life miserable. The wise man counsels us to exercise caution with these people and to learn what is appropriate and what is not (25:2–27).

The wise man prepares us to confront first the unpleasant men and women—the fool, the sluggard, the troublemaker, and the liar (25:28–27:4); then, as a second step, he deals with those who are supposed to be close to us, those we like naturally, our friends and our family (27:5–27).

What is not appropriate

The wise man explores various examples of misbehavior and denounces what is inappropriate. His first counsel is addressed to the future king, to warn him against presumption (25:2–3). It is not appropriate that the king identifies himself with God, as was often the custom in ancient Near Eastern culture. Israel was not a theocracy. While God's glory lies in His mystery, He is the God who hides His face (Isa. 45:14–15); the king's glory, in contrast, lies in his transparence and accountability to the people he rules over (Deut. 17:14–20). Consider the following paraphrased translation: "Hiding thing (impossibility to search) is the glory of God; but the possibility of searching thing is the glory of kings. Heavens are high above and the earth is down below; so is the heart of the kings; no need for searching there (it is exposed)" (25:2–3, author's translation).

The same language is used by the prophet Isaiah to describe God's prerogative: " 'For My thoughts are not your thoughts, nor are your ways My ways,' says the LORD. 'For as the heavens are higher than the earth, so are My ways higher than your ways, and My thoughts than your thoughts' " (Isa. 55:8). The practice of the leader to hide adultery or financial misdeeds is inappropriate. We are also told that it is not appropriate to practice boasting in the presence of the leader (25:6–7). Just as the king has to stay in his place before God, we have to stay in ours before our leaders. The child who addresses the adult, or the student who stands before his master, each one claiming that he knows better, are attitudes spoken against.

Also, it is not appropriate to blame our neighbor for a mistake and expose his case to the judge and to other people, at least without having first debated the matter with him (25:8–10). Jesus gives the same teaching, and He urges us to make every effort to first settle our dispute with our adversary before bringing the case to court (Luke 12:59). This reveals our fundamental duty to confront our neighbor about our problem before we go around and complain about him or her, and before our small amount of bitterness develops into irreversible hatred: "You shall not go about as a talebearer among your people. . . . You shall not hate your brother in your heart. You shall surely rebuke your neighbor" (Lev. 19:16–18; cf. Matt. 18:15). If we keep the matter in our heart, it will grow in our imagination; and if we share it with other people it will intensify and even take on disproportionate dimensions.

On the other hand, the sage of Proverbs emphasizes the appropriateness of "a word fitly spoken" (25:11). The wise compares the suitability of this word to the weather when it perfectly responds to the farmer's needs: "like the cold of snow in time of harvest" (25:13), or "cold water to a weary soul" (25:25). The counterpart of this experience is represented by the person who "falsely boasts of giving" (25:14). His words make us hope that money is coming, and nothing comes; this is "like clouds and winds without rain" (25:14). It is the same with the person who "bears false witness" (25:18). His words are as criminal as weapons. Trusting such a person is comparable to "a bad tooth" or "a foot out of joint" (25:19). You bite and your tooth drops. You walk and your foot stumbles. The unfitting is also "like one who takes away a garment in cold weather," or "like vinegar on soda" (25:20), or "a club, a sword, and a sharp arrow" (25:18).

Yet we should not abuse good words. The person who always says sweet things and always flatters will not be taken seriously. That person can come under suspicion. We should use good things with moderation. Do not eat too much honey, lest you become disgusted with it (25:16). In the same manner, we should temper our visits to our neighbor's house (25:17). As the old saying goes, "Familiarity breeds contempt." Also, "eating too much honey" is comparable to the person who seeks his own glory (25:27): his sweet words about himself will disgust people and will end with the opposite of glory.

This call for temperance continues in the next proverb (25:28), where self-control is commended. The person who cannot control himself is like an open city that lost its protective ramparts; the enemy will invade it and destroy it. When we lose our temper, we lose control of the discussion and, even if we are right, our opponent will inspire more confidence and will win the case. Paradoxically, it is appropriate to do good to our enemy; it is like heaping "coals of fire on his head" (25:22). The intention of this proverb is obviously not to hope harm for the enemy, as it has often been interpreted. The coals on the head of the enemy do not refer to the worst awaiting the enemy we have so treated. This image is supposed to convey a positive intention. Paul interprets it as an expression of love (Rom. 12:9–21). The image alludes to the Middle Eastern practice of carrying coals on one's head (in a basket) in order to fuel the fire of the hearth so that one may cook one's meal. To give food to the enemy is to provide him with the hope that he or she will still be able to eat later; it contains the possibility of peace between the antagonists.

Four portraits

The book of Proverbs contains a number of satiric portraits that are supposed to win the reader to the point of view of the wise man, who seeks to do this through humor and the evidence of vivid portraits. Laughter is sometimes more powerful than logical demonstrations. It is undoubtedly faster. Besides, it does not antagonize, because it is built on the basis of the common smile. These portraits are scattered throughout the book: the drunkard (23:29–35), the sluggard (6:9–11), the wicked man (6:12–15), the woman wisdom (8:1–31), the woman folly (9:13–17), the seductress (7:6–23), and the virtuous wife (31:10–31). In our current section of Proverbs, four portraits are grouped together to serve as the object lesson for the construction of wisdom.

The Fool (26:1–12). The point of this portrait is that there is no hope for the fool, just as there is no hope for any association with him. There is nothing good or right to expect from the fool. Just like snow in summer and rain in harvest (26:1), what the fool brings goes against what is normally expected. The fool is anti-hope. Therefore it is not appropriate to honor the fool (26:1b). Similarly, the fool is like "a curse without cause" (26:2); it does not make sense and there is nothing to expect from it (Num. 23:8). There is in fact more hope for the horse that responds to the whip or for the donkey that responds to the bridle than there is for the fool who would respond to none of them and who, in fact, needs a rod instead (26:3). It would not be wise to engage in discussion with him; otherwise we might end up sharing his folly (26:4). On the other hand, we should make sure that our silence will not encourage his folly (26:5); we should therefore find a good response to him and his foolishness. This contradictory counsel combines the force of silence, when our word is not needed, and the relevance of our word when we judge it necessary. Wise behavior is not mechanical but follows the nuances of life.

All of the following examples illustrate the anti-hope and anti-productive character of the fool. The fool is compared to a messenger without feet (26:6), the legs of the lame (26:7), and the binding of a stone in a sling (26:8). The portrait concludes with the tragic hopelessness of the fool, since he will continually repeat his folly "as a dog returns to his own vomit" (26:11). The fool will never learn the lessons of his folly. There is no hope for the fool because he thinks himself as wise (26:12). If, someday, the fool realizes that he is fool, then he will have taken the first step of his way to wisdom (cf. Dan. 4:34).

The Sluggard (26:13–16). A new image is presented to represent the sluggard. His turning in bed is compared to "a door [that] turns on its hinges" (26:14). The point of the parable is that the sluggard is fixed on the bed even when he moves. In spite of his motions, the sluggard does not make any progress in space. There is no difference between the sluggard and the fool; they both think of themselves as wise, with one little nuanced difference, however. While the fool simply thinks he knows, the sluggard thinks he knows *better* (26:16). Having thus solved all the problems by himself, and better than anyone else, the sluggard does not need to go elsewhere to learn or consult.

The Troublemaker (26:17–22). The person portrayed here is not clearly identified with a particular label. He is very busy interfering in disputes that do not concern him (26:17) and makes things worse (26:17). When people are in peace, he goes around agitating the various parties, and then, when faced with their anger, pretends that he was not serious about it and was only joking (26:18–19). In brief, this person is fueling the disputes (26:20–21). He claims that he meant to help the conflict; but he not only aggravated the present conflict but also created new ones. Those who were friends before are now fighting each other. Without his interventions, the quarrels would have calmed down and disappeared. The lesson here is to refrain from tasty and juicy gossip, easily swallowed and enjoyed but that goes deeply into the soul and corrupts the totality of the person (26:22).

The Liar (26:23–28). French novelist Albert Cohen described a genius as "someone who had his eyes full of wickedness while his heart was full of love."[1] The book of Proverbs describes the liar in exactly these terms: "fervent lips with a wicked heart" (26:23). While the former hides the good, the latter hides the bad. The liar's discourse is full of enthusiasm and passion about you or your work (26:23), but his heart is cold and is concerned with other things. In fact, he hates you and despises your work. He praises your book but does not care about it. He didn't even read it because he knew he wouldn't like it.

Two punishments await the liar. First, his lies will one day be publically denounced (26:26); that is, what was hidden will become common knowledge. Second, he will fall in his own trap. He will deceive himself and end up believing in his own lies (26:27). But this punishment and the disclosure of his real intentions will not come immediately. We are warned that, in the meantime, we should not be naïve; we should be lucid enough to discern hatred behind his lies and flatteries, and thus prevent the potential damage caused by what he says (26:28).

Friends and family

Before the discussion about those we love, the wise man lays down two fundamentals needed to preserve the quality of our relationship with them. First, we should not boast (27:1–2). It is not wise to brag

---

1. Translated from French by the author, from Albert Cohen, *Carnets 1978* (Paris: Gallimard, 1993), 54.

about what we plan to achieve and elaborate on our dreams for the future, especially when our friends and our family are struggling. Why should your friend who has been diagnosed with cancer hear you boasting about your great health? It is difficult for your friend whose spouse is sterile to hear you boasting about your children. It hurts the friend whose teenage son is a drug addict in prison to hear you boasting about the success and kindness of your children. The wise man warns us also that we do not know the future, and our present boasting may be contradicted by future events (27:1). It is therefore preferable to let your friend praise you (27:2). This friend's version of praise will not be done at his or her expense. Besides, someone else praising you is more believable than if it comes from "your own lips" (27:2b; cf. 27:21).

Second, we should beware of jealousy (27:4). Friendship should not be possessive. If we want our friend for us alone, we will lose that friend. This kind of friendship will generate destructive anger. We should love our friends and our family members for themselves and allow them to have interests other than ours, or to have other friends, even friends that you would not appreciate.

The Friend. The best demonstration of our friendship is not our approving silence or even our gifts at Christmas. It is the painful truth. When our friend behaves wrongly, when he cheats on his wife, or when he eats too much or drinks and destroys his health, then we should not forsake him, because a friend is often more valuable than a sister or a brother (27:10). The sister may be away or has simply lost contact with her brother and does not care about him because they do not share the same values. The friend, on the other hand, is presently near us, presently walking on the same path. We should have the guts to confront him with clear and unambiguous words. Our silence could be seen as an encouragement; it could even push him further on the way of death. It is better to speak clearly and openly with him about his misbehavior than to meet him with our embarrassed silence or with our subtle allusions (27:5). This kind of face-to-face encounter will strengthen the character of both friends, "as iron sharpens iron" (27:17). Both will come out better and greater from this difficult trial. These experiences will in fact be self-revelatory, just "as in water face reflects face" (27:19). It is therefore better to be wounded by a friend than to be kissed by an enemy, because the wound of the friend implies the truth and is meant for life, whereas the kiss of the enemy implies deception and is meant for death (cf. Mark 14:45). Ultimately, the heart-to-heart, tough confrontation will be like the sweetness of a perfume (27:9). On the other hand, the loud blessing of our friend is suspect (27:14). These ostentatious demonstrations may hide harmful intentions or are simply easy compensation for a shallow sentiment.

The Family. In Proverbs, the father has been asking his son to behave according to his instructions and to make his parents rejoice (1:8; 4:1, 20; 10:1; 15:20; 17:21; 23:22–25). Again the father begs his son: "Make my heart glad" (27:11). The father appeals to the love of his son in order to touch his son. Even if the son is not totally convinced of the wisdom of his father's recommendation, because he loves his father and mother he will consider it and do his best to please them. Education should be built on love and not just on principles. That the parents are right in their counsels to their children is important, but not enough to make their case through the heart of their children. On the other side, it is essential the son understand that it is his duty to make his parents glad, just as it was theirs to make him glad. It is that quality of the son's response to his parents that will ensure the happiness of his own family. A son who grew up in a loving family will, in his turn, generate a loving family.

From the call to rejoice in his parents, the wise man then moves to the next step, that is, to rejoice in his household (27:23–27). The good son will become a good father. The wise man conveys his teaching in a poetic language. Through the evocation of pastoral life, more than just the material needs of the sheep is implied. The point is that the son, who will be a father, must be fully aware of the needs of his house. The little details are listed. The father must take care of the hay, the tender grass, the lambs, and the goats (27:25–26).

Yet there is more here than the mere duty to provide for the physical necessities of our family. In the book of Proverbs, the Hebrew word *lekhem* for "food," is the technical term for "bread" (12:11). In addition to the "bread" (*lekhem*) that we bring to the table, the wise man refers also to *khayyim,* which means more than just "nourishment" (27:27). In the book of Proverbs, this term receives a strong spiritual connotation (10:11; 13:14; 14:27; cf. 3:2; 6:23). In a nutshell, he is responsible for the physical and spiritual survival of his family.

CHAPTER 11

A Lesson in Political Science

The field of political science, which is concerned with the running of government, has reached the conclusion that there is no such a thing as the "best government." Thomas Jefferson, the third president of the United States (1801–1809) and the principal author of the Declaration of Independence, concurred with this sad observation: "Experience hath shewn, that even under the best forms, those entrusted with power have, in time, and by slow operations, perverted it into tyranny."[1] All formulas have failed to bring happiness or to produce the perfect government on earth.

Biblical civilization is not an exception. From the time of anarchy under the judges, when "there was no king in Israel" and "everyone did what was right in his own eyes" (Judg. 21:25), to the hard years of nomocracy under the Law of Moses (Deut. 1:3; 6:1; 31:9), to the abuses of monarchy under the kings of Judah and Israel, there is always the same image: confusion. In this section of Proverbs, the wise man, himself a king, shares the same pessimism: "When the wicked arise, men hide themselves" (28:28). Under inspiration, and meditating on his own positive and negative experiences, King Solomon reflects on the

---

1. Thomas Jefferson, "Preamble to a Bill for the More General Diffusion of Knowledge," 1778.

responsibility of the leader and on his need for wisdom from above.

Two alternatives

We are faced with two alternatives: the bad one, how not to govern, and the good one, how to govern. In fact, the paradigm of these two models is illustrated in the history of kingship in Israel, which begins with a bad king, Saul, and a good king, David (see 1 Sam. 27–30). These first two reigns may well have inspired the political insights of Solomon, who rose immediately after them.

Thus, the wicked who flees for no reason (28:1a) could point back to Saul, who felt threatened by David, and yet David meant him no harm (1 Sam. 24:9). And the lion (28:1b) represents the righteous David, who rewarded Saul with good even though Saul rewarded him with evil (1 Sam. 24:17). It is interesting that the qualifying terms "wicked" and "righteous" are applied to Saul and David respectively in our passage (1 Sam. 24:13, 17). World history is full of these paranoid tyrants who fear everyone, even those who may support them. Hitler, Stalin, and more recently Idi Amin, Muammar Gaddafi, and Saddam Hussein were paranoid leaders who could not trust anyone and became the worst mass murderers of history. At the other extreme is the multiplication of weak rulers (28:2), a natural reaction that often follows absolute regimes, as is evidenced in the countries of these despotic leaders.

The need for Torah

From verses 3 to 12, the author of Proverbs builds a scaffold of parallels on the motifs. They follow like this:

A: Oppression of the poor (28:3)
  B: Forsaking the law (28:4)
    C: Evil men (28:5)
      D: Poor can be better than rich (28:6)
        E: Keeping the law (28:7)
A: Oppression of the poor (28:8)

B: Forsaking the law (28:9)
> C: Evil way (28:10)
>> D: Poor can be better than rich (28:11)

The lesson of this literary construction is centered on the principle of "keeping the law," the Torah (28:7). Those who forsake the law (28:4, 9) are in the camp of evil men, leading the righteous onto the evil way (28:5, 10). It is therefore better to be poor with "integrity" (28:6) and "understanding" (28:11) than to be rich with perversity (28:6) and wise in one's eyes (28:11). The mistake of this leader is that he values success and riches over integrity and true wisdom, and therefore oppresses the poor (28:3, 8). The wise man deals with the question of oppression. The oppressor commits injustice because of his ignorance or disregard of the divine Torah, which transcends and may even counter his personal ambitions and interests. The solution to abusive leadership is, therefore, essentially religious. It is related to the capacity to see and judge the situation, not from our limited and selfish angle but from the perspective of faith, which obliges us to see the other person in spite of ourselves. This capacity is "love" as the apostle Paul defines it: "Love does not envy; love does not parade itself, is not puffed up; does not behave rudely, does not seek its own" (1 Cor. 13:4–5).

The bad leader

The "poor man who oppresses the poor" (28:3) fits the description in Solomon's other book, when he talks about the poor, who "comes out of prison to be king" and yet oppresses his poor subjects (Eccles. 4:14–16; 1 Kings 11:40). This treatment is comparable to a driving rain that destroys everything (28:3). The poor who spoils the poor has forgotten his former condition and does not sympathize with the needy. Instead, he increases his riches at the expense of the poor (28:8, 15), and even of his parents (28:24). This kind of ruler is always associated with people who praise them (28:4); and so this ruler is reinforced in his injustice; he thinks he is right. These "evil men do not understand justice" (28:5). For the knowledge of justice is the capacity to discern what is just, and this discernment cannot be obtained through mere theoretical information.

However rich this ruler may be, he will not be able to think right because his knowledge of justice has been distorted by the way he runs his life (28:6). Indeed, the knowledge of justice is acquired only through the doing of justice and the keeping of God's commandments (28:7a). The paradox is that although he does not listen to the Torah, this person has religious behavior. For example, he prays (28:9), which is an insult to God (28:9b). Because of his powerful position as leader, he confuses the upright, who is then led astray (28:10). The weak Christian may sometimes identify truth with administrative power and believe that his or her leader must be right because he holds this high position, especially if this leader appears to be pious and prays beautiful prayers. Thus, such a ruler thinks of himself as wise (28:11); he covers his sins (28:13), and cannot therefore be forgiven (Ps. 32:5).

The result of this deepening in iniquity is that the leader "hardens his heart" (28:14); he pursues the politics of oppression and violence and, like King Nebuchadnezzar, he is identified as a beast lacking understanding (28:15–16; cf. Dan. 4:32). Although this wicked person seems to share the same fate as the righteous, since they both will fall and die, only the righteous will be saved (28:17–18). This leader is concerned only with easy pleasure (28:19) and the quick acquisition of wealth (28:20–22). He commits all these iniquities without any sense of guilt (28:24), and with a big ego (28:25),[2] trusting only in his own judgment (28:26). The bad ruler governs only from his own human perspective and seeks only his own interest. Paradoxically, this lack of generosity will not make him richer, unlike the one who gives to the poor (28:27). He rules to serve himself. This ruler takes advantage of his position of power to promote his family members or his close friends and to use the public funds for his personal projects.

---

2. The Hebrew *rekhab nefesh* means literally "large oneself," implying the idea of pride (cf. Ps. 101:5) rather than greediness (NLT, NIV).

A Lesson in Political Science

Three times in this section, like a refrain, the author emphasizes that a leadership of this sort of persons is unbearable to his subjects; when this kind of person comes to power, then the people hide (28:12, 28). They withdraw to their houses and live a private life without caring for their community; they do not vote, they do not express themselves, are no longer involved in the construction of the land, and fear for their security; or they simply go into exile and make their contribution there. Another unfortunate effect of this leadership is the loss of valuable people; the righteous disappear (28:28) and "the people groan" (29:2).

These scenarios have been observed in secular history; for instance, France lost many great minds during the religious persecutions of the Protestants; they fled to Germany and Switzerland and contributed to the prosperity there. The inspired writer of Proverbs predicts that this corrupt leader will reap his own iniquities; all he has earned from the poor will ultimately go to those who pity the poor (28:8), and he will ultimately "fall into his own pit" (28:10; cf. 29:5). In fact, their punishment is that "the righteous will see their fall" (29:16), and no one will help him (28:18). As for the societies that are under such bad leadership, they are bound to crumble (28:28b).

The specific cases of the antediluvian society (Gen. 4:5–6), of Sodom and Gomorrah (Gen. 18:16–33), and the Canaanite populations (Gen. 15:16; Deut. 18:9) come to mind. The total absence of righteousness results in total destruction. These dramatic examples anticipate the final end-time judgment, which points to the total destruction of evil (Rev. 20:7–10) in order that the kingdom of justice and peace may be established (Rev. 21:1–4). The salvation of the world implies, necessarily, the thorough cleansing of the world, the eradication of evil, as foreshadowed in the service of the Day of Atonement (Lev. 16:33).

The good leader

The counterpart of the bad ruler is delineated along the way in a contrasting picture. The good ruler is all that the bad ruler is not. While people groan under the wicked leader, people rejoice when "the righteous are in authority" (29:2). While the bad ruler is the companion of foolishness, which is personified by the harlot, the good ruler loves wisdom (29:3; cf. 7:10–23; 9:13–18). While the bad leader is corrupt, the good leader rules on principles of justice (29:4). While the bad leader enjoys flattery and falls in that trap (29:6), "the righteous sings [*run*] and rejoices [*smkh*]" (29:6). The same thinking is found in Psalm 92, which uses the same association of words: "For you make me glad [*smkh*] by your deeds, LORD; I sing for joy [*run*] at what your hands have done" (Ps. 92:4, NIV). While the wicked does not care about the poor, the good ruler considers the cause of the poor (29:7). While the scoffers bring conflict to the city, the wise men bring peace (29:8). While the wise man confronts the fool to reason with him, the fool does not listen; he either rages or laughs (29:9). While the wicked is subjective and governs according to his feelings and his personal affinities, the wise leader controls his personal sentiments and favors the righteous (29:10–11; 28:21). While the bad ruler "pays attention to lies," which may support his leadership (29:12), the good leader is concerned only with the truth, even if his government may be threatened by it (29:14).

Between these two proverbs about the bad and the good leader, the author inserts a paradoxical thought: the oppressing leader and the oppressed poor meet each other (29:13, RSV). This does not simply mean that they have something in common, namely the light that God gives to both (see 29:13, NKJV). No, the confrontation between these two enemies is also pregnant with the potential encounter of love between them. This is the difficult lesson that Jesus draws from the same meteorological observation: "But I say to you, love your enemies . . . that you may be sons of your Father in heaven; for He makes His sun rise on the evil and on the good, and sends rain on the just and on the unjust" (Matt. 5:44–45; cf. Job 25:3). While the good leader makes sure that evil is controlled and that wisdom is acquired through rigorous education (29:15a, 17), the bad leader does not control his children, bringing shame to their mothers (29:15b). While the wicked multiplies transgression (29:16a), the righteous waits in faith for their fall (29:16b).

Note the contrast between the febrile activism of the wicked, who counts only on himself and his politics, and the quiet assurance of the righteous, who has the faith that he will see the fall of the wicked and, hence, the victory over evil.

The need for prophecy

At this juncture, the wise man of Proverbs pauses to make a theological affirmation: "Where there is no revelation, the people cast off restraint" (29:18). For the first and only time, we are taken outside of the regular reflection of wisdom to a prophetic level. The wise man refers to prophetic revelation using the Hebrew word *khazon,* a technical term that designates the prophetic vision (Dan. 8:15; Jer. 14:14; Ezek. 7:26). The scope of the wise man goes beyond the usual individual application; it concerns more broadly "the people" (29:18a). He acknowledges explicitly the need of society for divine revelation. Implicitly this means that human wisdom, our philosophical, ethical, and political reflections and experiences, are just not enough. If we ignore supernatural revelation from above, we will have no restraint and no guidance. The wise man has in mind a people (our contemporary society?) who have lost the sense of evil and good; instead, they simply move and act according to their whim and opinion. These people are concerned only with happiness. Yet, emphasizes the wise man, the only way to be happy is not in doing what we want but in doing what God wants: "Happy is he who keeps the law" (29:18).

The following proverbs elaborate on this lesson. Attention to the law requires more than words (29:19–20); it is more than a theological essay or a spiritual sermon. It is more than a pious discourse. It must be translated concretely into our life, into our actions and our thinking. More precisely, the law deals with the way we treat others, such as our servants and our employees (29:21). It deals with the way we control ourselves (29:22) as well. The key for this whole operation is not, however, within our hands. Although it is made of our works, it derives essentially from our relationship with the Lord. Fearing humans is a trap (29:25a), and expecting justice from men is deceptive (29:26a). Only trust in the Lord is safe (29:25b), and justice comes only from the Lord (29:26b). Faith is the only answer.

Two incompatible worlds

The lesson ends, then, as it started: with the realization of two incompatible worldviews and mentalities. The just and the unjust are an abomination to each other (29:27). There is no peace possible between them, no compromise or middle way. It is a "perfect hatred" (Ps. 139:22). This stringent summation is the conclusion of the whole Hezekiah compilation of Solomon's proverbs (25:1–29:27). We are involved in a merciless conflict between good and evil, between the forces of God and the forces of the enemy. The apostle Paul reflects on this extraordinary character of the great controversy that concerns, this time, cosmic leadership: "We do not wrestle against flesh and blood, but against principalities, against powers, against the rulers of the darkness of this age, against spiritual hosts of wickedness in the heavenly places" (Eph. 6:12).

CHAPTER 12

Spiritual Battlefield

After the great Israelite kings, Solomon and Hezekiah, we are surprised to hear from an obscure pagan king, Agur, whose words, *masa'*, "oracle," and *ne'um*, "saying," are technical terms for prophetic utterances (Num. 24:3; Isa. 13:1). The prophetic revelation does not depend on ethnic culture or on education: "The wind blows where it wishes" (John 3:8). That the Bible records this manifestation of prophecy in a pagan context, along with the great oracles of the Hebrew prophets, paradoxically testifies to the divine authenticity of prophecy. Although Agur identifies himself as a prophet of God, he knows that something is missing in his knowledge of God. A literal rendering of his introductory phrase suggests that he even struggles with the idea of God. The Hebrew word *'itiel,* which has generally been understood as a person's name, "Ithiel," could also be read as an Aramaic phrase meaning "there is no God."[1] And the following, *we'ukal,* a phrase that has also traditionally been interpreted as referring to a person's name, "and Ukal," could also mean "and I prevailed" (cf. Gen. 32:8). The introductory line could then be translated: "Oracle of the man: 'there is no God, there is no God, and yet I prevailed' " (30:1b).

---

1. See R. B. Y. Scott, *Proverbs and Ecclesiastes,* Anchor Bible series (New York: Doubleday, 1965), 175–176.

Paradoxically, the prophetic oracle questions the existence of God, just as faith implies the struggle of doubt. Faith is belief in spite of doubt and not without doubt. These considerations may surprise or shock the common believer who has known God all his or her life. But we should remember that Agur is not a regular believer of our church or of our synagogue. He is not an Israelite; he is not a Christian. He comes from the pagan world and has no religious background. He himself recognizes his deficiency. In an oriental fashion he makes this self-derogatory confession emphatically. He is not just stupid; he is "more stupid than any man" (30:2). He then clearly identifies the nature of his ignorance. It is in the domain of theology: "I neither learned wisdom nor have knowledge of the Holy One" (30:3). In other words, Agur has no theological or confessional agenda. His message concerns everyone. Then, beginning with the cosmic scope of creation, he brings his cosmic lesson about the spiritual battlefield that involves all humankind.

From the cosmic scope of Creation

The poem evokes the four elements at the beginning of Creation: "heavens," "earth," "wind," "waters" (Gen. 1:1–2). Four times the same kind of question is raised: "Who has ascended?" "Who has gathered?" "Who has bound?" "Who has established?" And he ends with the question "Who knows?" (see 30:4). The language and style of the passage recall God's response to Job: "Who determined its measurements? . . . Who stretched the line upon it?" (Job 38:5). "Who shut in the sea?" (Job 38:8). "Who has divided a channel?" (Job 38:25). "Who has begotten the drops of dew?" (Job 38:28; cf. 38:36, 37, 41; 39:5). The discourse is also associated there with the question "Who knows?" (38:5, 20, 21, 33; 39:1). This parallel of Proverbs with the book of Job suggests that it is the divine Creator involving Jesus Christ as the divine Son who is implied in the questions "who?" and "what is His name, and what is His Son's name?" (30:4). As in the book of Job, God responds to someone who challenges His existence and His will.

Spiritual Battlefield

In consideration of the foreign origin of his testimony, Agur feels it necessary to emphasize the genuineness of the divine address: "Every word of God is pure" (30:5); even its canonic value is suggested through the use of a similar formula in other places of the Bible: "Do not add to His words" (30:6; cf. Deut. 12:32; Rev. 22:18). The universality of the word of God is affirmed: the God who speaks here does not depend on culture. And it is that God to whom Agur turns and prays. Agur introduces his prayer with his concern about the authenticity of his religious commitment: "Remove falsehood and lies from me" (30:8a).

Then, to ensure the quality of his religion, he asks God two things: "Give me neither poverty nor riches" (30:8b). Agur's point is that poverty as well as riches may be deceptive. Poverty may encourage unethical behavior and justify stealing. Too much riches, however, could cause him to turn away from God. In fact, the rich could even stop believing in Him. Thus Jesus warned: "It is hard for a rich man to enter the kingdom of heaven" (Matt. 19:23). There is something about the poor in his relationship with God that still demands respect. When we have everything we need, and believe in God, we should be careful not to judge the poor, who struggles with his Lord (30:10). Being in need, although problematic, keeps us closer to God than does being without need. Yet the wise man of Proverbs does not promote poverty as an ideal, since this condition can also take us far from God. In asking God to prevent him from having poverty or riches, the wise man is ensuring a scale of values that preserves faith. Our relationship with God is more important than what we have or don't have. Agur confirms, then, from his universal point of view, from outside of the particular tradition of Israel, the fundamental message of the book of Proverbs, namely that the fear of God is the beginning of wisdom (1:7; 9:10; 15:33; 31:30).

The Seven Wonders of the World

Agur then goes into another exposition. He is intrigued by five negative phenomena and two positive ones:

Proverbs

The Four Generations. Agur notes the progression of evil. What appeared to be a harmless behavior, cursing one's father and not blessing one's mother, is denounced as the root of evil. We begin with despising our parents, and we end in slaughtering and exploiting the needy. The loss of the sense of fatherhood leads to the loss of the sense of brotherhood.[2] When we eliminated the notion of respect and reverence toward our parents, who gave us life, and thus rejected the sense of mystery associated with those sentiments, we began shaping in our children the monster of their ego. This observation is particularly vivid in our modern societies, where the spoiling of children—along with the elimination of the respectful distance between parents and children—has produced generations of delinquency. It is no accident that the Bible sees in this phenomenon one of the signs of decay that characterize the end times (2 Tim. 3:2).

The Four Greedy Ones. From the lack of respect to our parents we move to never-satisfied avidity. There is an obvious connection between the two iniquities. The more we spoil our children and give them what they wish, the less we confront them with the reality that says "no," and the more they will be demanding. The image of the leech so eager to suck blood, and joined by its two greedy daughters, adds intensity to this activity. The opposite notions of death and birth and water and fire suggest this absolute character of greediness. The grave that swallows its ever-recurring dead, the barren womb that never gives birth, the earth that absorbs the always-renewing courses of water, and the fire that endlessly consumes everything—all share the same common hopeless prospect: the absence of life. This vision evokes the hopeless nature of the human condition. There is no way of stopping the process. In the book of Ecclesiastes, Solomon expresses his powerlessness at this phenomenon, which he calls "vanity" (Eccles. 1:2). Philosopher Albert Camus reflects on this character of life and refers to the ancient Greek legend of Sisyphus. It is the story of a god who was sentenced to

---

2. See Abraham J. Heschel, *Man Is Not Alone: A Philosophy of Religion* (New York: Farrar, Straus & Giroux, 1999), 112.

roll a boulder up to the top of mountain, only to have it roll down, only to have him push it back up, and so forth—an endless and meaningless process evoking the absurdity of our human condition.

The Four Stages of Contempt of Parents. Agur's oracle returns to his earlier warning about how we treat our parents, an indication of the importance he gives to this issue. The four stages parallel the previous progression, moving from mocking one's father and mother to the act of devouring others (30:17; cf. 30:14). This time, however, the tone of the oracle is threatening and sounds like a prophetic curse. The one who curses no longer devours but is himself devoured. Ironically, the eye of the cursing child, which thought of itself as wise (30:12), is now attacked by ravens and eaten by eagles. In passing, the oracle suggests that even if life seems to be unjust and allows the success of evil, there will be a judgment; the wicked will pay for their thoughts, words, and acts.

The Four Traces. From the eagles in the air, perhaps the same eagles that just ate the cursing eye, to the serpent on the rock, and to the ship in the sea, we come to the man with a woman (30:19). The idea is that none of these passing moves left any trace. The key of this riddle is immediately given: the adulterous woman claims her innocence since there is no trace of her adultery (30:20). The lesson of this natural observation concerns our struggle with evil and is related to the notion of the fear of God. When we commit iniquity in secret, we entertain the illusion that since no one saw us, we are innocent. Evil seems, then, to have triumphed since we do not feel guilty about it and are not even paying for it. This observation is congruent with the picture of the absurdity of life. Ecclesiastes pessimistically observes the unfair success of the wicked (Eccles. 3:16; 9:11). Agur resonates with this pessimism and is also perturbed by it (30:21): the servant who reigns (30:22a), the fool who is well fed (30:22b), the unloving woman who gets a husband (30:23a, RSV), and the maidservant who takes the place of her mistress (30:23b). These are all examples of this undeserved promotion.

Agur thinks that these cases of unfairness make the earth "shaken."[3] Faith in the justice of God and in Providence is thus challenged.

Four Illustrations of Faith. The next two wonders take us to the other side. The little things and the big things convey a double lesson of faith. The first series of examples, the ants, the rock badgers, the locusts, and the spider, speak of faith because they produce power against all expectations and show "the evidence of things not seen" (Heb. 11:1). Faith is belief that we are strong while we are weak (2 Cor. 12:10) because we trust that something powerful will come out of (and in spite of) our weakness. Faith is what made Abraham believe that he and his wife would have a child in spite of their old age (Gen. 15:6). Faith is belief that eternal life and glory will come out of the dust of death. Faith is what gives assurance to the prisoner Paul, who confronts the powerful king Agrippa (Acts 26:27–28). Agur is telling us through these parables, immediately after having listed the many evidences for the success of evil, that we can still believe in the victory of the good and that we can still hope in the kingdom of heaven, in spite of what we see here on earth.

The second series of examples—the mighty lion, the greyhound, the goat, and the king with his army—speak also of faith, but this time more directly: they epitomize the quiet confidence of the powerful. Agur is suggesting that, as men and women of faith, we are like the mighty lion and the powerful king. We should not fear or worry but trust our Lord, for our strength is precisely in that quietness (Isa. 30:15). These four examples are majestic in pace; they do not need to be agitated or to be quick. They have reached their peace, the *shalom* that makes them trusting in the outcome of the storm: "When the whirlwind passes by, the wicked is no more, but the righteous has an everlasting foundation" (10:25).

The oracle has just mentioned the "king whose troops are with him" (30:31). A literal translation suggests "the king, against whom there is no rising up" (JPS). The oracle pictures the threatening coming of God

---

3. This is the literal meaning of the Hebrew verb *rgz* ("perturb").

Himself, and addresses the wicked person who may be tempted to be foolish enough to brag about his wickedness and insist on planning evil. The wise man advises him to put his hand over his mouth, which denotes awe and astonishment (Job 21:5; Mic. 7:16) and staying silent. There is a literary play on the words "mouth" (*peh*), "nose" (*'ap*), and "wrath" (*'apayim*) to suggest some kind of connection between the three words. We had better shut our mouth and repent lest we are confronted in the ultimate and unavoidable dispute of the divine judgment. The Hebrew word *rib,* "strife," belongs to legal language and is often used to evoke God's dealings in judgment: "The clamor will resound to the ends of the earth, for the LORD has an indictment [*rib*] against the nations; he is entering into judgment with all flesh, and the guilty he will put to the sword, declares the LORD" (Jer. 25:31, NRSV; cf. Hos. 4:1; Mic. 6:1). The point of the oracle is not to scare anyone but to make the wicked realize their iniquity in the silence of their thoughts. The pressing of evil will produce anger, just as the pressing of milk produces butter, and the pressing of the nose produces blood (30:33). In other words, divine judgment is inescapable and—beyond the absurdities of human existence and human history—this prospect and promise gives sense to our life and to human history.

CHAPTER 13

The Acquisition of Wisdom

The book of Proverbs, which starts with the voice of a man, ends with the voice of a woman. If the name Lemuel, meaning "from God" or "toward God," refers to Solomon,[1] then it is David's wife, Bathsheba, who now instructs her son. In ancient Israel, wisdom was often associated with women, who were often consulted for advice (2 Sam. 14:2). The queen mother warns her son against the two things that may obscure his judgment and hence affect the quality of his leadership: wine and bad women. Solomon was tempted by wine, as the book of Ecclesiastes suggests (Eccles. 2:3), and was also influenced by women who will even trap him into idolatry (1 Kings 11:4). According to an old Jewish legend, Solomon got drunk at the celebration of his marriage with the Egyptian princess, and it was on that occasion that his mother reproved him (*Babli. Sanhedrin* 70b).

The last page of Proverbs is more, however, than a biographical note about Solomon. It is the last lesson of wisdom. It consists of warnings against women and wine that would prevent the ideal king from being wise and judging righteously (31:1–9). It is also a portrait of the ideal woman who embodies Wisdom and represents the ideal partner (31:10–31).

---

1. See *Leviticus Rabbah* 12.5; cf. Rashi in *Miqraot Gdolot* on Proverbs 31:1.

The ideal king

The queen mother begins her lesson with emotion. She introduces her discourse three times with the exclamation, "What?" And she repeats three times the word *son*. Her relationship with her son intensifies, from the neutral and legal address "my son," to the more physiological observation "son of my womb," to the loving confession "son of my vows" (31:2). It is on the basis of this precious bond that she builds her admonitions.

Beware of Women. The mother has nothing against women as a gender. Her language reminds us of the earlier lesson from the father who warned his son against the mortal danger of the immoral woman (5:3–14) and the harlot (7:26), who represented foolishness and evil (9:13–18). The mother is thus concerned with protecting her son against the influence of folly and the effect of iniquity, all of which may blur the king's judgment and duties as a king (31:3).

Beware of Wine. The queen mother is not just recommending temperance; she is not advising her son not to drink too much and not to get drunk. The parallel between the warning against wine and the warning against women suggests that the mother opposes wine just as she opposes women. She insists three times that it is not for the king to drink any kind of alcoholic beverage (31:4). The reason she gives reminds us of the reason given to justify the prohibition of alcohol to the priest; it has to do with the practice of the law and the application of justice: "lest they forget the law and pervert the justice of the afflicted" (31:5; cf. Lev. 10:9–11). On the other hand, and in contrast to the ideal king, she associates drinking with two categories of person: (1) the one "who is perishing" (31:6a), an expression that regularly stands for the "wicked" in the book of Proverbs (10:28; 11:7, 10; 19:9; 21:28; 28:28); and (2) the one who is "bitter of heart" (31:6b) that he may forget his misery.

It is not suggested here that the one who is depressed (the "bitter of heart") is allowed to get some drink. The fact that drinking leads to forgetting, just as is the case for the king who drinks and forgets the law, suggests that this forgetting should not be understood in a positive sense. Under the effect of alcohol, the "bitter of heart" will not only "forget his poverty"; he will also lose his sense of human obligation. The Hebrew word *'ml,* "misery," refers to the pain of hard labor (Eccles. 1:3). The point of the proverb is not that the drinking of wine will comfort the bitter of heart; the point is that he will no longer care for his misery and will, in the process, lose his sense of duty. Those who drink wine, the "one who is perishing" (wicked), as well as the "bitter of heart," are not models for the king, who instead should not drink wine because he has the double duty to "judge righteously" and to take care of "the poor and the needy" (31:9). The reason why the queen mother is so adamant against wine and the woman-folly is that they both affect the king's access to wisdom, his capacity to judge and to distinguish between good and evil.

The ideal woman

The Poem. What follows, the poem about the ideal woman, is not separated from the Lemuel text. It begins the same way, emotionally, and with a question: "Who can find a virtuous woman?" (31:10; cf. 31:2). On the other hand, the poem serves as the epilogue of the whole book of Proverbs. The poem is skillfully constructed as acrostic and chiastic. Acrostic: each line begins with a letter following the order of the Hebrew alphabet. Chiastic: the second part (31:24–31) mirrors the first part (31:10–22), with a distinct line in the middle (31:23):

A: Universal praise of the woman who is excellent (31:10)
  B: Husband needs her (31:11–12)
    C: The woman is industrious (31:13–19)
      D: The woman gives to the poor (31:20)
        E: The woman clothes her household (31:21–22)
          F: Her husband is honored (31:23)
        E': The woman clothes her household (31:24–25)
      D': The woman speaks with wisdom and kindness (31:26)
    C': The woman is industrious (31:27)
  B': Children and husband praise her (31:28–29)
A': Universal praise of the woman who fears the Lord (31:30–31)

Proverbs

The Ideal Wife. The first reading of the poem conveys the message of the ideal wife whom the wise son has to find in order to ensure a wise life in tune with the divine Law. Jewish tradition has retained this meaning; there is a Jewish custom for men to recite this text at the beginning of the Shabbat, as an expression of gratefulness for their wife. The point is that conjugal life is a part of religious life. Throughout the Scriptures, the woman and the conjugal metaphor illustrate the adventure of God's relationship with Israel. In that other book written by Solomon, the Song of Songs, a beautiful poem about human love, the poem refers also prophetically to God's relationship with His people. The most immediate lesson for the son of Proverbs is to understand that his spiritual destiny depends on the choice of the right woman and on the quality of his relationship with her. When he finds her, he finds wisdom and experiences the presence of God Himself.

The Qualities of the Woman. What singles out this woman is not found in her appearance, in her charm or in her beauty (31:30), but in her spiritual nature: she "fears the LORD" (31:30); she is wise and kind (31:26), and she anticipates the "time to come" (31:25). But she also thinks concretely and confronts reality: she works hard day and night (31:15, 18), brings food (31:15), buys a field (31:16), and plants a vineyard (31:16). But more important, she is characterized by what she does for others, first for her husband, who appears symmetrically in the beginning (30:11), at the end (31:28), and in the center (31:23); then for her children (31:28–29), her maidservants (31:15), and the poor (31:20). She is not even aware of her qualities. The recognition of her virtue comes from the outside, and the testimony is universal (31:10, 31). In fact, her works speak for her (31:31). This portrait may shock feminist advocates who may see here an apology for the woman serving for the benefit of the male. But this is not the point of the poem, which, incidentally, may have been written by a woman (Lemuel's mother). The intention of this portrait is to suggest the ideal of wisdom as a ministry of service. Wisdom is not this magic power that will make us superior and thus served by the others. Wisdom is the capacity to serve others.

The Acquisition of Wisdom

The ideal that is suggested here concerns men as well as women.

The Divine Presence. A number of clues in the language of the text and the specific context of Proverbs indicate that the "virtuous woman" is the embodiment of wisdom, and not just the ideal wife. Thus, the description of this woman echoes many passages in the book of Proverbs referring to Wisdom. She possesses the "fear of the LORD," the fundamental requirement for wisdom (1:7). Like in many passages in Proverbs, the good woman represents wisdom (1:20–33; 3:13–20; 4:5–9; 8; 9:1–6). It is also significant that wisdom is represented by a woman of divine nature in Proverbs 8, with all the qualities we find in the ideal wife of Proverbs 31. She is worth being found (31:10; cf. 8:35); she provides wealth (31:11; 8:10–11, 18) and food (31:15; cf. 8:19); she is strong (31:17; 8:14); she is a blessing (31:28; cf. 8:32); she is praised (31:28; 8:34). Also, the central message of the poem, as suggested through its chiastic structure, is a veiled exaltation of God, the honored husband who reigns "among the elders of the land" (31:23). Wisdom is compared to the ideal wife because wisdom is not just an intellectual acquisition. We reach wisdom through the process of a relationship with the divine person. The book of Proverbs concludes, then, with this parable, the last *mashal;* it is an appeal to the reader to go and search for Wisdom and engage in a dynamic conjugal relationship with her, to make our life meaningful and full of the divine Presence.

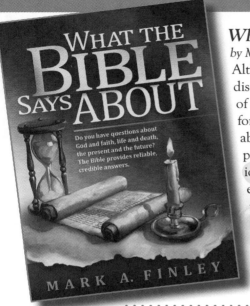

What the Bible Says About
by Mark Finley

Although God's Word touches on a variety of disciplines, it is first and foremost a revelation of God's will, revealing His eternal truths for the human race. Do you have questions about God and faith, life and death, the present and the future? Rather than opinions or sermons, *What the Bible Says About* is especially designed to give you answers directly from Scripture. Allow God's Word to answer your deepest questions and speak to your heart's deepest needs.

Hardcover, 528 Pages
ISBN 13: 978-0-8163-3403-2
ISBN 10: 0-8163-3403-X

Journey Through the Bible
by Ken Wade

Journey Through the Bible is a map to the Book of books. Like any good map it provides an overview that will help you know what to look for as you search for God's guidance through the Word. In these three volumes, with clear insight, author Ken Wade helps you grasp the central message of each book, from Genesis through Revelation.

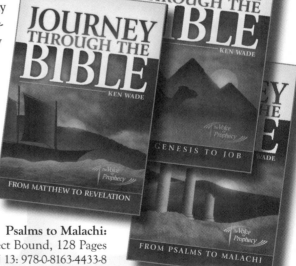

Genesis to Job:
Perfect Bound, 160 Pages
ISBN 13: 978-0-8163-4309-6
ISBN 10: 0-8163-4309-8

Psalms to Malachi:
Perfect Bound, 128 Pages
ISBN 13: 978-0-8163-4433-8
ISBN 10: 0-8163-4433-7

Matthew to Revelation:
Perfect Bound, 160 Pages
ISBN 13: 978-0-8163-3940-2
ISBN 10: 0-8163-3940-6

Pacific Press®
Publishing Association
"Where the Word Is Life"

Three ways to order:

1 Local	Adventist Book Center®
2 Call	1-800-765-6955
3 Shop	AdventistBookCenter.com